Competency–Based Training Basics

William J. Rothwell
and
James M. Graber

Ed Pauzer
NYCDOC Academy
66-26 Metropolitan Ave
Middle Village, NY
718 417 2340

ASTD
PRESS

Alexandria, Virginia

© 2010 American Society for Training and Development, William Rothwell, & James Graber

All rights reserved. Printed in the United States of America.

16 15 14 13 12 11 10   1 2 3 4 5 6 7 8 9 10

No part of this publication may be reproduced, distributed, or transmitted in any form or by any means, including photocopying, recording, or other electronic or mechanical methods, without the prior written permission of the publisher, except in the case of brief quotations embodied in critical reviews and certain other noncommercial uses permitted by copyright law. For permission requests, please go to www.copyright.com, or contact Copyright Clearance Center (CCC), 222 Rosewood Drive, Danvers, MA 01923 (telephone: 978.750.8400, fax: 978.646.8600).

ASTD Press is an internationally renowned source of insightful and practical information on workplace learning and performance topics, including training basics, evaluation and return on investment, instructional systems development, e-learning, leadership, and career development. Visit us at www.astd.org/astdpress.

Ordering information: Books published by ASTD Press can be purchased by visiting our website at store.astd.org or by calling 800.628.2783 or 703.683.8100.

Library of Congress Control Number: 2009925588

ISBN-10: 1-56286-698-2
ISBN-13: 978-1-56286-698-3

ASTD Press Editorial Staff:
Director of Content: Adam Chesler
Manager, ASTD Press: Jacqueline Edlund-Braun
Project Manager, Content Acquisition: Justin Brusino
Senior Associate Editor: Tora Estep
Associate Editor: Victoria DeVaux
Editorial Assistant: Stephanie Castellano

Editorial, Design, and Production: Abella Publishing Services, LLC
Cover Design: Ana Foreman

Printed by Versa Press Inc., East Peoria, IL, www.versapress.com

Contents

About the
Training Basics Series

■■

ASTD's *Training Basics* series recognizes and, in many ways, celebrates the fast-paced, ever-changing reality of organizations today. Jobs, roles, and expectations change quickly. One day you might be a network administrator or a process line manager, and the next day you might be asked to train 50 employees in basic computer skills or to instruct line workers in quality processes.

Where do you turn for help? The ASTD *Training Basics* series is designed to be your one-stop solution. The series takes a minimalist approach to your learning curve dilemma and presents only the information you need to be successful. Each book in the series guides you through key aspects of training: giving presentations, making the transition to the role of trainer, designing and delivering training, and evaluating training. The books in the series also include some advanced skills such as performance and basic business proficiencies.

The ASTD *Training Basics* series is the perfect tool for training and performance professionals looking for easy-to-understand materials that will prepare non-trainers to take on a training role. In addition, this series is the perfect reference tool for any trainer's bookshelf and a quick way to hone your existing skills.

Preface

Competency-Based Training Basics is intended to be a practical primer on competency-based training and learning. It is meant to help trainers and managers achieve better results through greater awareness and use of competencies. Knowing what makes some individuals more productive than others is fundamental to effective management and deployment of workplace training and learning programs.

The book is written for anyone who facilitates learning or guides training and development. This audience includes

- learning and performance professionals
- managers
- HR professionals
- subject matter experts.

Trainers are steeped in the theory and practice of the instructional systems design (ISD) model. Central to that model is analyzing the work that people do, which includes evaluating the tasks they perform to achieve results. Learning professionals have traditionally given less credence to the importance of the unique characteristics of the most successful or even outstanding performers. Yet, understanding these differences is extremely important to your organization's overall business health. Many learning professionals and their sponsoring organizations are now rethinking traditional learning approaches and placing greater emphasis on individual differences to achieve desired business results. Increasingly, trainers must understand the use and deployment of competency-based learning to successfully plan for and facilitate new or existing learning events and training programs. Tapping into innovative ways to build a workforce populated by top performers is one of the principal goals of this book.

Unfortunately, few trainers or their managers have any formal training on the complex topic of competencies or competency modeling, no matter the pedigree of their college or graduate degrees. This organizational reality is a business miss for many companies since managers (who increasingly are taking on more training responsibility) are the natural choice to be the coaches and mentors who might convey these basic principles to their teams.

Competency-Based Training Basics is a first step toward making a vital competency knowledge connection that has a direct link to efficient business operations. Ninety percent of competency development occurs on the job, which means that the principles and practices described in this book are critically important for supervisors, managers, and even top talent management executives who must find, develop, and retain those who possess achievement-focused competencies. For learning professionals willing to invest the time, this book provides the informational building blocks needed to fully tap the potential of these powerful business tools.

Chapter-by-Chapter Highlights

Each chapter in this book is intended to contribute to your success. Here is a summary of the chapters:

Chapter 1: What Is Competency-Based Training? The terminology used to explain or identify the concepts behind competency-based learning differs from organization to organization. This chapter clarifies terminology to provide a common understanding.

Chapter 2: Why Organizations Use Competencies. Not all organizations are convinced that using competencies is a good idea. This chapter makes the business case for using competencies.

Chapter 3: Basics of Assessing Competencies and Determining Learning and Training Needs. This chapter provides a detailed look at how to assess the competencies of individuals and groups in organizational settings. Practical advice is given for keeping the assessment process simple and manageable while producing adequate information for individual development and other purposes.

Chapter 4: Designing Training Using Competencies. Chapter 4 explains how the traditional ISD model must be modified to use competencies in training and facilitating learning.

Chapter 5: Using Technology to Support Competency-Based Learning. This chapter identifies both the benefits and the challenges of using technology for competency management. It describes how technology may be used as a tool—but not a crutch—for competency identification, modeling, assessment, and talent management.

Chapter 6: Communicating About Competency-Based Approaches. Competencies are often developed and deployed before users even understand what competencies are and why they are beneficial for the organization. Communicating and selling the value of competency-based approaches to key stakeholder groups is covered in this chapter.

Chapter 7: Using Competencies to Guide Learning—An Application Guide. This chapter focuses on the "how to" of competency-based learning. It examines two common scenarios faced by learning and performance professionals. The first scenario offers guidance to learning professionals who are asked to integrate a set of competencies (developed by someone else) into their training programs. The second scenario provides advice on how to link an existing slate of learning events and programs to a new competency model.

Chapter 8: The Future of Competency-Based Training and Learning. The final chapter offers ten predictions for competency-based training and learning in the future.

The book ends with two appendices, including useful competency sources and references.

Appendix A: Frequently Asked Questions (FAQs) About Competency-Based Training. A focus group of the Chicago chapter of ASTD provided source material for these FAQs. Use the FAQs as a handout in your training department or management kickoff meetings where competency-modeling projects are to be launched or in training sessions to brief trainers, executives, managers, or front-line supervisors about competencies. The FAQs should address many of the typical questions that managers and workers may ask.

Appendix B: Competency Modeling: The Basics of Identifying Competencies. Identifying competencies and building competency models is a large enough topic to warrant its own book. This appendix gives you a base knowledge of the process of developing a competency model. It summarizes various approaches to building a library of competencies that are relevant to an organization. You will learn, at a high level, three approaches that are comparable to the "make," "buy," and "buy and modify" approaches to obtaining competency models. It distinguishes core, cross-function (or "generic"), and specialty ("functional" or "technical") competencies and approaches for identifying each. It discusses approaches for identifying behavioral statements that further define competencies, as well as behavioral questions for selection purposes. For examples of competency models, visit www.astd.org/CompetencyBasedTrainingBasics.

Look for These Icons

What's Inside This Chapter

Each chapter opens with a summary of the topics addressed in the chapter. You can use this reference to find the areas that interest you most.

Think About This

These are helpful tips for how to use the tools and techniques presented in the chapter.

Basic Rules

These rules cut to the chase. They represent important concepts and assumptions that form the foundation of virtual training.

Noted

This icon calls out additional information.

Getting It Done

The final section of each chapter supports your ability to take the content of that chapter and apply it to your situation. Sometimes this section contains a list of questions for you to ponder. Sometimes it is a self-assessment tool. And sometimes it is a list of action steps you can take to enhance your facilitation.

Acknowledgments

William J. Rothwell dedicates this book to his wife, Marcelina Rothwell, and to his daughter, Candice. They light up his life.

James M. Graber dedicates this book to his father and mother, who have served as world-class role models, and to his wife, Pamela, and two daughters, Brittany and Grace, who epitomize what is important in life.

James would also like to thank the following individuals (primarily from the Chicago chapter of ASTD), who provided many of the questions appearing in the FAQs in Appendix A: Jennifer Everett, Kirk Hallowell, Connie Hinkle, Matt Hoff, Julie Jacques, Anu Khetarpal, Deborah Lopuszynski, Catherine Marienau, Nancy Moran, Jerry Mount, Deborah Pastors, and Dirk Tussing.

We would also like to thank Mark Morrow for his patience and encouragement to write this book. William J. Rothwell would also like to acknowledge the contribution of his hardworking graduate assistant, Aileen Zabellero, who helped secure necessary copyright permissions for this book when needed.

William Rothwell
James Graber
October 2010

What Is Competency-Based Training?

What's Inside This Chapter

In this chapter, you'll learn

▶ What competency-based training is
▶ Basic definitions of key competency terminology.

Whether you are building training and learning competencies from scratch or deploying predefined competencies, the job requires a mastery of various terms and concepts. The technical details are complex, so we present the definitions of the key competency terminology in the simplest terms possible.

Defining Competency

The term *competency* refers to any characteristics of an individual performer that lead to acceptable or outstanding performance. *Competencies* may include technical skills, level of motivation, personality traits, awareness of bodies of knowledge, or just about anything else that can assist in producing results. Competencies are the domain of individuals; thus, it is important to remember that analysis of successful performers is one of the best ways to isolate and identify qualities that make some people more successful than others.

Developing a Competency Model. A *competency model* is a set of competencies (typically 10–30) that describe the capabilities of successful performers. Competency models are derived by focusing on the behavior of successful performers instead of only examining or relying on the knowledge, skills, and abilities (KSAs) related to a list of tasks. Competency modeling begins by establishing profiles of *ideal performers*—that is, those who are the most effective as defined objectively by measurable work standards. Any difference between an ideal performer and other performers is called a *gap* and usually is expressed in behavioral or work output terms. Developing a competency model can be complex and laborious and is not normally a function of trainers. However, to better understand competency models, a complete explanation of competency modeling is offered in Appendix B.

Competency-Based Training

Competency-based training is intended to help individuals acquire or build the necessary characteristics to match the skills of good or exceptional performers. This book will show you how to understand and deploy a competency model in your organization's learning and training events.

Note, however, that not all competencies can be developed in individuals and, for instance, competency-based training doesn't necessarily guarantee a successful employee; even a precise set of salesperson competencies will not necessarily allow you to turn introverts into great sales professionals.

Basic Rule 1

Do not confuse competencies with job descriptions. A *job description* describes the work the individual is expected to perform; a *competency model* profiles the shared characteristics of people who perform the work successfully or outstandingly.

Competency-Based Learning

Although trainers, facilitators, or managers can provide experiences that build desired competencies, increasingly, the primary responsibility for *competency-based learning* rests with learners. Assertive learners seek out people or experiences that will help them remain employable, qualify for promotion, transfer to another department, change careers, or move to another organization. The difference between competency-based learning and competency-based training is that competency-based training is sponsored by organizations to help individuals match profiles of ideal performers, whereas competency-based learning is undertaken by individuals who are motivated to align themselves with good or excellent performers.

Key Terms

The following terms are intended to help you take maximum advantage of this book. These are very basic explanations; for more detailed or technical explanations of competencies, see the appendix.

Job competency—As defined by Boyatzis (1982, p. 20), this means "an underlying characteristic of an employee (that is, motive, trait, skill, aspects of one's self-image, social role, or a body of knowledge) which results in effective or superior performance in a job."

Organizational capabilities—The essence of what makes an organization competitive or successful. For a business, this refers to the unique and key strengths that make one business different from, and superior to or distinguishable from, its competitors.

Cross-functional competencies—Common competencies that may be shared by a variety of workers; for example, project planning, time management, budgeting, or writing skills.

Technical or functional competencies—Unique knowledge essential to work in a functional area (such as engineering).

Core competencies—A limited list (usually 4–7) characteristics deemed by an organization to be especially critical and pertinent for all levels and functions of an organization. For example, learning agility, working effectively with others, or integrity.

Competency modeling—The process of discovering competencies.

Competency assessment—The process of comparing an individual to a competency model.

Competency development—The building of competencies, which usually occurs through job training, formal education, networking, or on-the-job work experience. Developmental experiences are usually focused on building competencies as assessed at the behavioral level using an array of resources including books, e-learning, training programs, work experiences, or other efforts.

Competency acquisition—The process by which an organization acquires competencies. Methods for acquisition include building them within the current workforce, hiring them from outside, or a combination of the two. Increasingly, organizations are "renting" them by relying on contingent workers, vendors, consultants, or outsourcing.

Competency-based training—The process of building competencies that align with strategic organizational success or job success.

Competency model—A set of competencies (typically 10–30) that describes the capabilities of successful performers.

Behavioral indicators—The behaviors associated with a competency in an organizational culture. See the example in Exhibit 1–1.

Behavioral anchor—Behaviors that are arranged in order of preference for performance, usually based on research about what behaviors are more often demonstrated by the best performers compared to average or subpar performers. For an example, see Exhibit 1–2.

Exhibit 1–1: Sample Behavioral Indicators

Customer Service

Definition: Understands that all state employees have external or internal customers that they provide services and information to; honors all of the state's commitments to customers by providing helpful, courteous, accessible, responsive, and knowledgeable service.

Indicators for a Successful Performer

Willingly provides assistance and useful information to meet customer needs; takes appropriate actions to provide accurate information to customers; assumes ownership of customer issues and takes appropriate steps to correct problems.

Source: Georgia's Behavioral Competency Dictionary State Personnel Administration – 2008. www.spa.ga.gov/pdfs/wfp/GA_framework.pdf

Exhibit 1–2: A Sample Behavioral Anchor

Adaptability

Maintaining effectiveness when experiencing major changes in personal work tasks or the work environment; adjusting effectively to work within new work structures, processes, requirements, or cultures.

Needs Improvement

- Displays resistance and is uncomfortable with change. Does not cope well with change.
- Continues to rely on existing approaches and procedures.
- Portrays a negative attitude toward change as well as those implementing the changes. Does not see the benefit in change and anticipates the worst.
- Unnecessarily questions change.
- Does not accept or support the overall vision for the department.
- Does little or nothing to help subordinates accept change.

Meets Expectations

- Attempts to understand changes in work tasks, situations, and environment as well as the logic or basis for change. Sets goals and priorities to accomplish change.
- Promotes and encourages change. Does what is necessary to adjust to change for self and others.
- Sees where change benefits the organization and the people in it.
- Deals effectively with changes in direction.
- Directs and assists subordinates through the change process.

High Performing

- Anticipates work changes and quickly adapts to the new situations and work requirements. Actively seeks information regarding new work situations.
- Approaches change in a positive manner. Handles change and new situations as opportunities for learning or growth and focuses on the beneficial aspects. Speaks positively regarding change to others. Sets a strong example for staff.
- Envisions the end results of change and follows through to ensure that changes are properly integrated and performed.
- Excels in an environment of frequently changing work structures and processes. Takes appropriate risks in order to implement change.
- Champions change. Supports subordinates' work as change agents.

Source: State of Michigan, *Supervisor Competencies Rating Scales*. www.michigan.gov/documents/ group3SupvBARS_42992_7.pdf

Work outputs—When associated with a competency, these are the results of demonstrating a competency.

Quality requirements—A measurement of the quality of work output.

As you read this book, these definitions will become more a part of your vocabulary. You might want to bookmark these definitions for future reference. In the next chapter, you will learn how and why organizations use competencies.

 Getting It Done

This chapter emphasized the difference between descriptions of work and descriptions of the people who successfully perform the work. Here are some questions to help you develop a mindset for the application of the principles you will learn in the succeeding chapters:

1. Consider how competencies influence your daily work. Can you list some ways this influence is manifested?
2. George is a very talented engineer who graduated with high honors from a well-rated university. However, he has not performed nearly as well as most other engineers at his current employer. While the talent is evident, which other competencies might be missing?
3. What is the focus of traditional training? How could you explain to operating managers the difference between traditional and competency-based training? How would you explain the difference to workers?

2

Why Organizations Use Competencies

 What's Inside This Chapter

In this chapter, you'll learn

▶ Why organizations are strengthened by using competencies
▶ Why learning and performance professionals benefit from using competencies as a basis for training and development.

Knowledge of competencies and competency modeling is increasingly important for workplace learning professionals tasked with learning results. Most front-line learning and performance professionals and their managers have encountered competencies or competency modeling in their careers, but few of these professionals have had any formal training on these topics.

Our goal is to address this deficiency so that you can put these powerful, productivity-enhancing tools to work in your organization.

Why Competencies Are Important to Organizations

Research suggests that some individuals may be 20 times more productive than others. Clearly, any CEO would welcome as many of these individuals into an organization as could be mass produced. Matching individual competencies with job competency models puts individuals in positions where they can contribute most. Competency learning cannot promise a 20-fold increase in productivity, but it will move people in the right direction.

Think About This

How do people discover their special talents? Why do some people get better results than others even though they share the same job title?

If developing talent is critical to the future success of organizations, then understanding and using competencies to create a more talented workforce is key to maintaining a competitive edge. Learning and performance professionals have an important role to play in this future success through the use of competencies.

Competencies in Organizations

Competencies are not about duties, they are about people. In that respect, they are different from job analysis (a process) and its traditional output (a job description). Theoretically, all HR efforts should be based on job descriptions. Unfortunately, job descriptions focus on the work, not on the unique characteristics of people who are successful doing the work. As a result, job descriptions often fail to address measurable results; and since job descriptions are based on activities or duties, they may change quickly as organizations recognize work assignments or change how the work is done.

As an example, consider the job description of an executive assistant. A typical work activity on a job description might read, "types letters, reports, travel vouchers, and other documents." But that description of an activity does not indicate how many letters, reports, travel vouchers, or other documents are actually produced, how much of the work involves typing, how critical typing is to overall job success, and what measures are used to determine success in that activity.

Competencies are more enduring than job tasks. Competencies focus on the characteristics of people who are successful performing the work. Competencies are part of people, not the work they do. Competencies do better in pinpointing the unique characteristics of people that lead to success. This has been overlooked or poorly identified in most traditional job descriptions, which typically have a brief list of knowledge, skills, and abilities that may not be specific to the job and may only cover technical skills.

As a simple example, a job description for a janitor might indicate that a successful applicant would possess a high school diploma. It might further indicate that job incumbents should "know how to operate floor polishing machines, use a broom and a mop." It might go further and indicate that "the janitor is willing to take initiative." But of course, these requirements provide little information about what is really needed to perform this job successfully. For instance, what competencies can we assume are present in a high school graduate and how many are really necessary to do this job?

Organizations that understand the characteristics of those who get the best results develop a competitive advantage. They are better positioned to recruit, select, develop, reward, and promote the most successful people. Hence, competencies are an important tool, much like a compass, to find direction in attracting, developing, retaining, and positioning the best, most productive and promotable people. In this regard, competencies are the "glue" that holds talent management programs together.

For example, ABC Corporation manages a chain of fast food restaurants. Several years ago, ABC developed competency models for all positions in the restaurant, such as cooks, counter personnel, and people at various levels of supervision and management. Now when hiring, they use the competency models to guide their behavioral interviews. Competency gaps identified during the hiring process help to determine appropriate individual development plans. Staff who are motivated to move up in their jobs work to develop competencies required by more advanced, higher-paying positions.

Competencies support organizational capabilities. Successful organizations possess capabilities that differentiate them from the competition and help them achieve strategic objectives. For example, organizations can excel at innovation, reliability, efficiency and low cost, or speedy delivery of services. These organizational capabilities must be supported by the right collective mix of competencies. Strategic objectives imply that some competencies will be needed more than others to achieve results. Organizational leaders can operationalize strategy by clarifying what competencies are needed to achieve future strategic objectives. For example, XYZ Corporation manages homes for senior citizens. XYZ has identified core competencies and values that are key to its growth strategy and are required of all associates. These include compassion, communication, and customer focus.

Closing Gaps and Leveraging Strengths

A *job performance gap* occurs when someone does not meet the requirements (competencies) for his or her current level of responsibility. A *development gap* occurs when someone does not meet the requirements (competencies) for higher-level responsibility. Learning and performance professionals assess individuals against the competency requirements of a position and pinpoint areas requiring development. Once gaps are identified, a plan can be prepared to close them through a performance management plan or an individual development plan. Whereas the performance plan might outline detailed action steps to guide improved performance, an individual development plan will focus on competency development.

An alternative to focusing on gaps is to discover the strengths of individual performers and leverage this strength for advantage. Individuals who exceed the requirements for their current level have *performance strengths.* Individuals who exceed the requirements for higher levels have *development strengths.* Strengths can be leveraged by positioning people where they can best use their strengths and serve as mentors for others needing to close performance or developmental gaps.

Competencies make gaps and strengths measurable and identifiable for action. Thus, competencies are useful whether a professional prefers to close gaps or leverage strengths—or do both.

Why Learning Professionals Should Use Competencies

Whether the goal is to narrow a performance or developmental gap or to leverage a performance or developmental strength, competencies can be useful to learning and performance professionals for several reasons:

> ▶ **Competencies pinpoint what is important.** By studying those who get good results and what makes them able to get those results, learning professionals can focus training or even create a developmental strategy. If it

is true that most development occurs on the job, then training is only one way to build competencies. Other ways to build competencies include receiving coaching from one's supervisor, networking with peers, watching strong performers, accessing a knowledge database that provides standard operating procedures or information on how similar issues have been handled successfully in the past, participating in a problem-solving group, joining a community of practice, or using more traditional approaches such as reading books and articles or watching DVDs or online videos.

▶ **Some organizational leaders believe that developing people requires attention to a 70–20–10 percent rule.** According to that view, 70 percent of all competencies should be developed through real-time, on-the-job experiences that are intended to build the competency; 20 percent of competencies should be developed through networking with associates in person or online (such as communities of practice or using Web 2.0 technology); and only 10 percent of competencies should be developed through planned training. For example, suppose a manager wishes to develop an individual's competencies in budgeting skills. Training is only one way to do that. A more effective way might be for the manager to assign the person to work on a current department budget with the coaching of the manager. The manager may identify others in the organization who do a good job in budgeting and ask the person who is being developed to approach those people for advice either through face-to-face meetings or by virtual interaction.

Basic Rule 2

Follow the 70–20–10 Rule: 70 percent of competencies should be developed on the job, 20 percent through networking and collaboration, and 10 percent through planned training.

▶ **Competencies can tie training to other HR efforts.** As common denominators, competencies help describe what abilities the organization needs and how to acquire them. Competencies can be part of employee hiring, on-boarding, performance appraisal, compensation, and succession planning.

▶ **Competencies can make it easier to communicate with workers about the qualifications needed to be considered for future work in the organization.** With competency models, individuals are given ways to assess themselves—or involve others in providing valuable feedback. Multi-rater, 360-degree feedback assessments are frequently used for this purpose, particularly for soft skills, but increasingly for feedback on technical performance or skills. Individuals gain information that can be used to compare their own competencies to those required for other positions within the organization. Individuals receive valuable feedback for improving their readiness for more advanced positions and thus furthering their careers. Competencies provide a means to discuss career paths and articulate specific ways to develop oneself or leverage one's strengths.

Getting It Done

This chapter explained why organizations are using competencies. Here are some questions and suggestions to help you apply what you learned.

1. Prepare a one-minute talk, suitable to deliver on an elevator ride, to explain to a manager why an organization should use competencies.
2. Create a list of why individuals should care about competency-based learning. How might it relate to career goals?
3. The chapter noted that many organizations are striving for a learning mix of 70–20–10: 70 percent of learning on the job, 20 percent learning through coaching and collaboration, and 10 percent in formal learning settings. Explain what implications that might have for your organization. Also explain how competencies might be used as the blueprint or basis by which to organize learning experiences.

3

Basics of Assessing Competencies and Determining Learning and Training Needs

What's Inside This Chapter

In this chapter, you'll learn

- ▶ How competency assessment is done
- ▶ How to use the results of competency assessments to create individual development plans (IDPs) to narrow performance or development gaps and to leverage personal strengths.

Assessing Competencies and Prioritizing Needs

To assess competencies, learning and performance professionals, not just performance professionals, must work with a competency model that is measurable. A *measurable competency model* identifies the competencies of the position or job, as well as the behavioral indicators, behavioral anchors, or work outputs and quality requirements. (See chapter 1 for an explanation of these terms.) Most often, learning and performance professionals will be given competency models by consultants or by HR professionals—or perhaps even by corporate headquarters. Your task is to use the established model to assess individual workers and to compare the results to the model. This process allows identification of the worker's performance gaps and strengths. (But if you are given the challenge of building a competency model, see Appendix B).

Common Types of Assessments

Here are six types of assessments you are likely to encounter as a training professional. Note that each has its own special strengths and weaknesses.

Self-Assessments

A *self-assessment* allows individuals to evaluate themselves against a competency list with behavioral indicators, behavioral anchors, or work outputs. If an organization has completed job-specific competency models, an individual may have the option of choosing one or several assessments of greatest pertinence to his or her career interests from a large library of assessments. A tool for reflection, self-assessments are useful because they can give individuals clues about their areas of strength or weakness. An advantage of this approach is that it is fast and does not require much data gathering or number crunching. A disadvantage is that the results may not be all that accurate because the data reflect only the viewpoint of one person. See Exhibit 3–1 for an example.

Manager Assessments

Manager assessments are evaluations of a manager's direct reports. The competencies included in the assessment come from a relevant competency model (for current job or future jobs of interest). Once the manager completes the assessment of the individual, the results are useful for creating targeted individual development plans and for selecting current or future work assignments. Like a competency self-assessment, an advantage of this approach is that it is fast (it can usually be completed within 30 minutes) and with supporting technology can be done with little or no administrative effort. A disadvantage, like the self-assessment, is that the results represent only one of many possible perspectives. Depending on the types of competencies being assessed, this can be a significant limitation. For example, if teamwork is a required competency, wouldn't it be valuable to hear from peers that have been teammates? (See Exhibit 3–2.)

360-Degree Assessments

Sometimes called a multi-rater, full-circle assessment, a *360-degree assessment* collects data in a full circle around an individual. The assessment may be based on a general (for example, leadership) or job-specific competency model. These 360-degree assessments have become a well-accepted, widely used measure of competencies in part because of the inherent attractiveness of comparing different perspectives to one's self-rating. Although not easy to administer, a 360-degree assessment is simpler to develop than some of the other ways of measuring competencies, such as skill tests, assessment centers, and certifications. Using competencies as measured by behavioral indicators or work outputs with quality requirements, individuals are asked to rate themselves.

Exhibit 3–1: Sample of a Self-Assessment Format for Competencies

Directions: For each competency and each associated behavioral indicator, rate yourself on how well you believe you can demonstrate the behaviors linked to the competencies. When you finish your assessment, forward it to the appropriate people in your organization according to the instructions they give you.

How well do you feel that you can demonstrate the following behaviors linked to the competencies?

Competencies/Behaviors	Rating				
	0	1	2	3	4
Competency: Writing skills	Not Applicable	Not Very Well	Not Well	Well	Outstanding
1. Effectively organizes written material					
2. Uses effective grammar					
3. Spells properly					
4. Gears the language to the appropriate level of the audience					

Exhibit 3–2: Sample of a Manager's Assessment Format for Competencies

Directions: For each competency and each behavioral indicator linked below, rate one employee on how well you believe he or she can demonstrate the behaviors linked to the competencies. When you finish your assessment, forward it to the appropriate people in your organization according to the instructions they give you.

How well do you feel that the employee can perform the following behaviors linked to the competencies?

Competencies/Behaviors	Rating				
	0	1	2	3	4
Competency: Writing skill	Not Applicable	Not Very Well	Not Well	Well	Outstanding
1. Effectively organizes written material					
2. Uses effective grammar					
3. Spells properly					
4. Gears the language to the appropriate level of the audience					

At the same time, other people—such as an immediate supervisor, peers, subordinates, and possibly internal customers, external customers, and suppliers—are also invited to rate the individual's competencies. An average score is then calculated for each group. Some 360-degree reports provide scores for each respondent group, and some combine all the respondent groups into one rating to compare to self-ratings.

An important assumption of the 360-degree assessment is that greater objectivity can be gained when an individual's self-rating is compared to the average of others. According to Max DePree in *Leadership Is an Art* (2004), every person is really three people: (1) the person you think you are, (2) the person others think you are, and (3) the person you really are. By comparing self-ratings to ratings by others, individuals can discover the mysterious "person others think they are" and compare that to the "person they think they are." This can lead to profound conclusions and possibly motivate people to narrow performance or development gaps. It may also suggest strengths that can be advantageously leveraged for oneself and others.

A further advantage of a 360-degree assessment is that it can reveal blind spots (the classic example is the supervisor who incorrectly believes his direct reports appreciate his management style) or suggest areas for improvement. It can also provide information from more than a single source, revealing different realities (for example, an individual may communicate well with peers but not with his or her boss). One possible disadvantage of a 360-degree assessment is that it is subject to a variety of rater errors (for example, "halo effect"or "horn effect" in which one good or bad deed can exert excessive influence on an assessor). Another possible disadvantage is that not all raters are equally capable of rating people on behaviors linked to competencies because some raters (such as customers) have infrequent or highly focused contact with workers and may not observe the full range of behaviors that the individual performs.

180-Degree Assessments

A *180-degree assessment* collects data in a half-circle around an individual. Using competencies as measured by behavioral indicators, behavioral anchors, or work outputs with quality requirements, individuals are asked to rate themselves. At the same time, other people—typically an immediate supervisor and several subordinates only—are invited to rate the individual's competencies.

Some organizations prefer the 180-degree assessment over the 360-degree assessment because it takes less time and less administrative effort. A disadvantage is that important perspectives may be left out.

Assessment Centers

An *assessment center* provides an environment in which simulation of the work is performed. First, a job study is conducted to identify what individual performers do and the results they achieve. Next, raters are selected and trained to evaluate others. (Sometimes the raters have performed the job.) The raters observe the worker perform the simulation(s) and then provide ratings based on the observed behaviors or the work outputs produced as measured against the previously identified requirements. Assessment centers have been frequently used to measure teamwork and leadership skills. When making selections of executives, or when assessing the development needs of executives, assessment centers are often useful.

One advantage of carefully designed assessment centers is that these centers can quickly and realistically simulate work environments in one or more critical areas without the risks that the work might be performed incorrectly in the regular work environment. Assessment centers can provide highly valid and repeatable ratings that can be consistently applied when comparing different employees. However, assessment centers can be expensive to develop, and the use of observers can be time consuming and costly.

Certifications

Increasingly, organizations are asking supervisors or subject matter experts (SMEs) to verify (or certify) the competencies of employees. Other certifications are conducted by evaluators outside the organization, but in either case, the supervisor or SME must be given the proper verification tools.

The first step in the process is to define desired learning outcomes. Requiring learners to understand certain terminology, know safety requirements, identify different components used in a process, or understand reporting requirements are all examples. When the learner is ready to be assessed, the observer watches and evaluates the performance using a pre-developed rating sheet. The observer may be required to ask a set of critical questions but may have the leeway to selectively verify other outcomes. If employees are successful, they receive positive feedback and the observer signs off on the certification. If employees are not successful, they receive positive but corrective feedback and follow-up actions are prescribed. This approach can provide valid and reliable evaluations. It can easily be tailored to the specifics of the organization, and employees generally see it as fair and constructive. However, more upfront work is required than for 360- or 180-degree ratings, and the approach is likely more practical when a large number of employees are required to demonstrate the same competencies.

Think About This

Remember that a competency model describes "what should be" and an assessment identifies, for an individual, "what is." Can you think of other approaches to competency assessment? If so, what might be their advantages and disadvantages?

Noted

Creating a Positive Learning Climate

A positive organizational climate is essential for the successful development and deployment of competencies. For example, if workers fear the loss of their jobs, those needing development may not request development or admit to any shortcoming. Managers may also hold off requesting further development since admitting any shortcoming in their performers may be seen as reflecting on the manager. If you think this dynamic exists in your organization, a climate assessment may be in order (Rothwell, 2002). The assessment tool illustrated in Exhibit 3–3 can be used for this purpose. Administer the instrument separately to managers and workers and present the results back to both groups. Some basic questions to ask include:

(1) Why did the organization score as it did with each group?

(2) What can be done to improve the learning climate in the organization?

(3) What roles and accountabilities should each worker and manager have for developing themselves and others?

You can use these questions as a launching point to build efforts to improve the positive learning climate of the organization.

Using Assessment Information

Regardless of how an individual is assessed, a competency assessment should result in a follow-up (typically a development plan). The assessment report should indicate competency scores, and it may even produce a list of specific behavioral indicators tied to the competencies for individuals to develop or strengths for individuals to leverage. It is important that the list be prioritized because individuals rarely have time to work on developing more than two or three competencies at one time. Sophisticated competency models that have different weights for more important competencies and different desired levels of competency performance depending on job requirements can lead to a list of prioritized development needs included with the assessment report. Once development priorities are agreed upon, individuals and their supervisors can collaborate to create an appropriate individual development plan.

Competency Assessment and Individual Development Plans

The development of an IDP is related to the topic of competency assessment. Competency identification produces a competency model. Competency assessment compares an individual to a competency model and produces a list of behaviors or outputs that the individual needs to develop or strengths the individual can leverage. An IDP produces an action plan to narrow or close performance/development gaps and leverage individual strengths.

Most IDPs cover at least the following elements:

▸ name of the person for whom the IDP is being developed

▸ contact information of that person (phone, email, fax)

▸ name of the person's supervisor

▸ time period covered

▸ list of competency areas/behavioral indicators to be addressed (derived from the competency assessment)

▸ list of learning objectives, derived from the list of competency areas/behavioral indicators to be addressed

▸ list of actions to be taken and development resources to be used (for example, e-learning, books, activities, and so on) to meet the learning objectives

▸ time line for completion

▸ method of measuring or assessing individual competency-building efforts (outcomes of development)

▸ estimated budget for the IDP to be completed (optional).

Think About This

Even if two individuals intend to develop the same competency—for example, presentation skills—it doesn't follow that the development plan will be the same for both individuals. What factors might result in two individuals developing their presentation skills differently? An *Individual Development Plan* (IDP) is an action plan intended to help individuals narrow performance/development gaps or to leverage their individual strengths.

How IDPs Are Created

People who are being assessed are sometimes asked to complete the first draft of an IDP. As part of that process, these individuals may be asked to consult an online or print development resource guide (described in the next section of this book) to identify the most feasible approaches to building the competencies that the assessment has pinpointed. After the IDP draft is completed, individuals meet with their immediate supervisor to discuss the plan. The same approach may be used for narrowing or closing either performance or developmental gaps.

If a strengths-based approach is used, individuals may be asked to assess their strengths, perhaps using a self-assessment instrument, and then meet with their immediate supervisor to discuss ways to leverage the strength(s) to the advantage for themselves and others.

IDPs are sometimes included as part of a performance management form. But they may also be managed separately from the performance review process and thus stand alone. Operating managers often favor combining the two forms so that one meeting can measure an individual's present job performance and identify individual development needs. But a disadvantage of that approach is that it leads to confusion. Is all development meant to rectify performance deficiencies? The authors of this book would argue that is not the case. But combining the performance review and the process of developing the IDP can lead some managers and some workers to that point of confusion.

Learning and performance professionals can use IDPs as a way to individualize development requirements, using competencies as the foundation. Learning professionals can then "roll up" the individual IDPs to detect shared needs across many employees, thereby making it easier to pinpoint group learning needs aligned to the organization's strategic direction. Learning professionals can also identify development needs that are unique to individuals.

Getting It Done

This chapter focused on assessing competencies and using them to identify learning needs. Here are some questions to help you apply what you learned.

1. Describe what you believe to be the appropriate role of the manager in assessing competencies and identifying learning needs. How can managers be prepared to enact their role successfully?

2. How should an organization's leaders set priorities on meeting learning needs?

Exhibit 3–3: Sample of an Assessment Instrument for Learning Climate

Directions: Use this instrument to assess the learning climate in the organization. For each item in the left column below, rate it in the right column using the following scale:

1 = Strongly disagree

2 = Disagree

3 = Agree

4 = Strongly agree

When you are finished, add up the score below.

Do you supervise other people in this organization?   Yes ( )   No ( )

Characteristics of the learning climate	Rating of the climate			
In this organization, workers...	1	2	3	4
1. Are encouraged to build their knowledge and skills to solve real-time problems they face	1	2	3	4
2. Are given the time they need to build their competence so that they can solve problems they face	1	2	3	4
3. Are given the resources they need to build their competence so that they can solve the problems they face	1	2	3	4
4. Believe that their immediate supervisors will make time to coach them to solve problems	1	2	3	4
5. Believe that their immediate supervisors make time to coach them building their knowledge and skills to meet future work-related challenges	1	2	3	4
6. See a clear relationship between what they learn and the work problems they face	1	2	3	4

Exhibit 3–3: Continued

Characteristics of the learning climate	Rating of the climate			
7. Are encouraged to apply on the job what they learn in training off the job	1	2	3	4
8. Feel their coworkers will help them learn new things of use in solving work-related problems	1	2	3	4
9. Feel that they will have a greater chance of being rewarded if they learn new things of value to their work	1	2	3	4
10. Feel that they will have a greater chance of being promoted in the future if they learn new things of value to their work	1	2	3	4
Score	**Add up the scores from the columns.**			

Cash $10

HEY AMERICA!
WANT A FREE CLASSIC DONUT WHEN YOU
PURCHASE A MEDIUM OR LARGER BEVERAGE?
Go to www.telldunkin.com on your
computer or mobile device in the next
3 days and tell us about your visit.
Te invitamos a participar en
nuestra encuesta.

Survey Code: 54301-51655-1303-0471

Enter Validation Code:
Bring receipt with code to redeem
offer in store.
Visit DunkinDonuts.com for
redemption restrictions.
Franchisee: Please use PLU #201

****
Try Sweet and Salted Cold Brew.
A new signature beverage featuring
Dunkin's ultra-smooth Cold Brew,
sweetened with liquid cane sugar &
topped with an irresistible
salted whipped topping.
****

Thank You Come Back Again

4

Training Using Competencies

■ ■ ■ ■ ■ ■ ■ ■ ■ ■ ■ ■ ■ ■ ■ ■

...ide This Chapter

...ou'll learn

...ining methodology (ISD model)

...ompetencies related to the
...ction.

...sign Model

...cribed in many ways, but most of those ways
...ated by the 10 steps below, presented with a
few basic notes.

Step 1: Determine how much of a performance problem can be solved by training
and how much must be solved by alternative actions by management.

  ▶ Training should be conducted only when the problem stems from
    deficiencies of individual knowledge, skill, or attitude. If the problem stems,

in whole or part, from other sources, then management action will be necessary. Management controls the environment in which workers do their jobs. *Management action* includes changing selection methods, changing job descriptions or work requirements, changing performance review criteria, changing tools or equipment given to workers, and changing reward or pay systems.

Step 2: Determine measurable work requirements and assess how well workers are meeting those requirements.

  ▶ Steps 2 through 5 are focused on *training needs analysis.* If training can solve a problem, then it is important to target who will receive the training, what they need to do, and in what setting or under what working conditions they will perform. If training needs analysis is performed improperly—or if it is skipped completely—then there is a good chance that the training will not focus on the right issues.

Step 3: Examine the conditions under which workers will apply what they have learned from training.

Step 4: Become familiar with the background of the workers who will participate in training and determine what they already know.

Step 5: Clarify the specific gaps in knowledge, skills, and attitudes that training will address.

Step 6: Determine the desired outcome of training in terms of what participants should know, do, or feel upon completion of training.

  ▶ *Instructional objectives* describe what learners should know, do, or feel upon completion of training. *Performance objectives* describe what learners should know, do, or feel on-the-job after training is completed. Good objectives are clear, measurable, and achievable.

Step 7: Determine how learning (instructional objectives) will be measured.

  ▶ Testing methods should be established before training is designed and delivered so that tests will hold learners accountable for achieving the required objectives. Will workers be given tests of knowledge, or will they be asked to demonstrate their performance?

Step 8: Establish the instructional content necessary to achieve the objectives.

▶ Where will the training material be found? Will it be modified from existing content, created, or bought?

Step 9: Assess the most effective means to deliver the instructional content to the learners.

▶ Will the training be classroom-based training, online learning, on-the-job training, or a blend of available options?

Step 10: Determine how training results will be measured when the learner is back on the job (performance objectives).

▶ Donald Kirkpatrick's four levels of training evaluation have been widely used to measure training impact. They include the following:
  1. Reaction: How well did participants like the training?
  2. Learning: How much did participants learn?
  3. Behavior: How much change occurred back on the job as a direct result of training?
  4. Results: What measurable results did the organization obtain as a direct result of training?

▶ Alternatively, training's impact could be measured vis-à-vis an organization's annual goals or balanced scorecard. For example, an organization might have financial, employee development, continuous improvement, or innovation goals. Measuring training against organizational goals helps to ensure that training is focused on organizational needs and has a strategic impact.

Modifying the ISD Model to Use Competencies

Using a set of competencies to develop training or learning events does not require a great deal of change to the familiar ISD model. You can follow the process steps for the traditional ISD model with the changes and additions noted below. Steps 1–4 are the same as the traditional ISD model, so the discussion relating to competencies begins with Step 5 and the changes that need to be made. Note that there are two additional steps in this process.

Step 5: Determine who the most productive performers in the organization are and what characteristics they have in common.

▶ The organization's leaders need to identify the most productive performers. It is important to note that this does not mean identifying the managers' favorite people. Measurable performance—*objectively measured*—should be the basis for identifying top performers. If it is not possible to use measurable productivity standards, then it will be necessary to either establish them first and then find the best performers or else poll current job performers about who they believe to be the top performers and why they believe these people perform so well. Some competency experts suggest that job incumbents, more than immediate supervisors, are the best judges of who are the best performers if objective criteria for performance are lacking.

Step 6: Compare the most productive performers to acceptable (average) performers to determine what individual characteristics set them apart. What makes the top performers, called *exemplars,* different from the acceptable performers? Some of these differences may be traceable to individual strengths, whereas other differences may stem from knowledge of the best ways to get the work done (so-called tricks of the trade). Study superior performers to find out what makes them able to obtain better results than others. Does superior performance have something to do with the person—such as a unique talent with mathematics—that makes the person get such good results in a job that requires mathematics? Alternatively, the individual may have learned unique ways to become more productive—for instance, a top-performing salesperson may be top-performing precisely because she knows how to get around individuals whose goal is to screen and can therefore directly reach decision-makers who can sign contracts. Acceptable performers may have not learned how to do that.

Step 7: Determine how competencies will be measured. Should behavioral indicators be used? Or maybe skill tests or certifications? Should work outputs be used along with quality requirements? You should involve training sponsors to make this determination.

Step 8: Identify competencies the participants should be able to demonstrate upon completion of training.
  ▸ Objectives should be stated in competency-based terms. Specifically, knowledge and performance objectives state the desired results in terms of what competencies the training is intended to build and how those competencies will be measured.

Step 9: Determine how training results will be measured.

Step 10: Source the instructional content needed to build essential competencies.

Step 11: Determine the most effective means to deliver the instructional content to the learners.

Step 12: Plan how to measure training results upon completion of the training and when applied back to the job.

Think About This

This chapter explained that exemplars differ from acceptable performers in that they get results more beneficial to the organization. As noted, one reason exemplars get better results has to do with individual talents. Other differences may stem from "working smarter" based on experience or learning. Clarify what you think "working smarter" might mean. *Hint:* Think about how workers discover "work-arounds" to red tape.

Developing Workers Using Competencies

Using competencies expands the range of learning methodologies beyond training. Some alternative learning methods are listed below:

- reading articles or books
- accessing internal databases of best practices or other relevant knowledge
- using external websites
- watching DVDs or listening to audio files
- receiving coaching from inside or outside the organization
- participating in organizational work experiences
- observing and emulating outstanding performers
- visiting or spending time at centers of excellence inside or outside the organization.

Competency Development and IDPs

Using competencies also expands the range of development options for IDPs. For example, development resource guides (DRGs) are developed based on an organization's competency models. The DRG is a comprehensive guide, available to all employees and their managers, that suggests appropriate training resources for developing the organization's competencies. A more complete DRG will list a variety of resource mediums (for example, books, e-learning, on-the-job training, and so on) for each competency to accommodate different personal preferences of learners. The resources should also span the spectrum of basic to advanced to accommodate the differing starting levels of employees.

DRG resources usually include commercial content such as articles, books, DVDs, audiotapes, websites, conferences, external training seminars offered onsite or online, and even university course offerings. DRGs are also related to specific corporate resources that are unique to an organization. These may include internally developed and delivered classroom training, individual coaches, places where the competency is demonstrated properly, suggested work assignments, internal websites or resources, and electronic performance support systems that provide on-the-job, context-sensitive coaching tips or tools that help individuals to perform effectively. Some organizations may also opt to purchase access to commercially developed and maintained databases (for example, databases of training offerings) or to bring in consultants to develop content for the organization's DRG.

Other Uses of Competencies

Competencies are the common denominators that can tie together all elements of HR systems. Organizational leaders may use competencies as a basis for assessing which candidates to recruit and select, how to train, how to develop, how to manage or appraise performance, whom to select as successors, how to promote, how to reward, and even whom to transition out of the organization. Competencies, when measurable through behaviors or work outputs, become a foundation for planning for talent, building talent, and acquiring talent. Although this book is not about other elements of HR (Dubois & Rothwell, 2004), it is important to emphasize that competencies can be the basis for transforming the HR function beyond mere competency-based training.

Getting It Done

In this fourth chapter, you learned about how to define competency-based training, what enhancements are needed to apply competency-based training to the traditional ISD model, how competencies may be used in developing workers, and how competency-based training relates to other key components of HR systems.

Working off the common belief that the best way to learn something is to teach it, prepare a brief presentation on the topics presented in this chapter and share it with learning and performance professionals or operating managers in your organization.

- ▶ How would you apply the ISD model to competency-based training in your organization?
- ▶ If you were developing a DRG of competency-linked resources, what competencies would receive priority in your organization? What would be the ideal mix of resource types, including traditional training, collaboration and networking, and on-the-job learning?

5

Using Technology to Support Competency-Based Learning

What's Inside This Chapter

In this chapter, you'll learn

▶ The benefits and challenges of using technology in competency-based training
▶ The role of the competency-based trainer in developing learning resources that are accessed by individuals on a just-in-time, as-needed basis.

Studies by ASTD and others confirm the rapidly increasing role of technology in learning. Technology can play a particularly large role in organizations that embrace the 70–20–10 approach to learning and as learners take on more responsibility for their own learning.

In the context of competency-based learning, *technology* can be defined as tools and platforms that augment the learning processes. Technology offers excellent solutions for competency identification, modeling, and assessment. In addition, it provides a platform for efficient creation and delivery of competency-based learning. The combination of growing learning needs for individuals and organizations due to ever-increasing business and environmental changes together with the trend toward fewer support staff, including training staff, requires getting more done with fewer resources. Technology can help fill the gap.

However, technology also brings risks and challenges. Key obstacles are

▶ lack of internal technology expertise
▶ too few learners to justify a technology solution
▶ insufficient financial resources to cover initial costs of technology acquisition and implementation
▶ training and change management before a technology solution can be successfully implemented
▶ circumstances better suited to traditional low-tech learning methods
▶ if technology is substituted for qualified, effective training and development staff or for poor learning processes within your organization.

Technology presents challenges, but it is becoming increasingly difficult each day to imagine a competency-based training approach without new learning technologies as a crucial component. This chapter offers advice to help you maximize the rewards of technology while minimizing the risks.

Basic Rule 1

Technology allows the competency-based trainer to magnify his or her results. Do not assume, however, that you can go out and buy any learning technology that will "run on auto-pilot" and provide the quality learning your organization needs. Technology is like an "empty glass," and your organization must supply the content that will make it worthwhile. You will also need to maintain, enhance, and update that content. A lot of effort and organization will be required.

How Technology Strengthens Competency-Based Learning

Technology offers the opportunity to increase the effectiveness of virtually all aspects of the learning process, including creating, publishing, delivery, and maintenance; but its impact on how learning occurs is probably most obvious. It is at the foundation of a rich new stew of learning opportunities such as social networks, communities of practice, learning on demand, and mobile learning (to name a few), which brings many benefits:

- ▶ Technology-based learning can be blended with traditional training to increase training impact and improve transfer of new competencies to the work environment.
- ▶ As we have pointed out previously, competency-based learning focuses on the individual and what he or she can do to make an increased contribution. Technology will allow you to cost-effectively make available a variety of individualized learning opportunities.
- ▶ Technology offers the opportunity for employees to learn and grow almost every day, rather than confining learning to a few days or weeks of formal training each year. Clearly, more growth can occur when continuous learning takes place.
- ▶ Technology enables employees and their supervisors to take on increasing responsibility for learning. The individualized, tailored development can increase learning and learning return-on-investment, and build the commitment to learning for supervisors and employees.

Noted

In the technology-driven learning environment, learning professionals transition from "trainer" to "learning broker." Although they may continue on occasion to personally deliver training, trainers bring their skills to bear on creating learning environments designed to provide learners with quick access to a variety of useful learning resources.

How You Can Leverage Learning Technologies

Learning technology can be used in many different ways, and its benefits to you will vary based on the learning requirements in your organization, as well as what work is done internally and what is outsourced to external providers.

Consider which of the following might be advantageous to you and your organization:

▶ *Rapid creation of high-quality learning content.* Training that might have required several months to develop in the past may now be created in several weeks through leveraging re-usable content and efficient tools for creating e-learning.

▶ *Simplified training development tools that allow SMEs to develop some training.* Given that SMEs are the most important source of information about required competencies, a tool that allows them to record their knowledge in a training-ready format can save a lot of time and can quickly expand organization-specific training offerings that can be made available.

▶ *Tools that ease the process of testing and evaluating individual learning comprehension (Kirkpatrick's second level of learning evaluation) and competency acquisition.* It is beneficial to have better data on the effectiveness of training as well as better knowledge of individual competence. Imagine the value of knowing that 98 percent of staff has successfully mastered information on a new legal requirement or a new product or service. Imagine being able to concentrate on the 2 percent that haven't absorbed the new information. Testing also increases individual accountability for training results. When individuals share accountability, they will be more motivated to increase competence.

▶ *Providing on-demand access to formal and informal training materials.* Any organization with staff in different locations and time zones will benefit greatly from easy, 24/7 learning access available anywhere an Internet connection is available. Imagine the cost savings from reduced travel and the benefits from not having to present the same training numerous times.

▶ *Social learning, coaching, and collaborative learning.* Competency trainers are actively building this element into training to simultaneously make it more effective and more engaging, while helping build work relationships that individuals can leverage long after the training is complete.

▶ *Managing bodies of knowledge.* For example, suppose you are building the competence of staff to provide effective customer support. Imagine the value of being able to leverage an online database of previously reported issues and see how similar problems were solved in the past by exemplary performers. The database may also provide insights into occasions when customer problems were not handled effectively. Just having such a database as a resource that already exists and that continues to improve over time can also prove beneficial to a competency-based trainer.

▶ *Enabling learners to manage their own training.* This includes self-assessments, finding learning resources or information, creating development plans, requesting and working with mentors, collaborative learning with peers, and so on. Given that ever fewer organizations have structured, step-by-step career paths, and given that career development is increasingly tied to individual competencies, it is no longer practical for training staff to own accountability for career planning. It is essential that competency-based trainers be able to offer tools and guidance that allow individuals to play a more active role in their development.

Technology Related To ASTD Areas of Expertise (AOEs)

The ASTD Workplace Learning and Performance (WLP) Competency Model (see Appendix B Exhibit 5) identifies nine different areas of expertise in which learning professionals may be asked to perform. These are

1. career planning and talent management
2. coaching
3. delivering training
4. designing learning
5. facilitating organizational change
6. improving human performance
7. managing the learning function
8. managing organizational knowledge
9. measuring and evaluating.

Regardless of your job title, be it training manager, organization development specialist, organization effectiveness consultant, or other, competency-based training will require that you perform many of these roles. Although technology can be applied in any of these AOEs, we focus next on six of the roles where you are most likely to benefit from applying technology.

Career Planning and Talent Management AOE

The global recession of 2007–2010 may have reduced the need in some organizations to recruit new talent, but shortages of skilled labor have continued, for example for U.S. and U.K. employers (Randstad Human Capital Survey, December 2008). Meanwhile, increased pressure on the bottom line has further increased the need to improve employee performance. Those organizations that are adept at maximizing the contributions of their entire workforce, not just a few "stars," will flourish. It is especially critical for competency-based trainers to learn to develop talent/competencies on a daily, real-time basis (Rothwell, 2010).

Think About This

We are willing to bet that your organization has a full plate of learning-related priorities that would be worthy of your attention and financial resources. Should implementing technology be a top priority? Evaluate the importance of each of the following possible benefits for your organization to help you decide:

- reducing facility and travel costs associated with training

- providing flexible learning options for a diverse employee population from four generations or with diverse learning styles

- having learning available for more competencies (maybe ten times as much as you have today)

- shortening the time between learning request and learning delivery, perhaps to just a few days

- permanently capturing learnings, posting them, and re-using those learnings in new training offerings in the future

- identifying learning needs more accurately

- quicker preparation and deployment of new employees

- better measuring and reporting on the impact of learning.

Three primary trends are driving the practice of career planning and talent management:

1. Previously, HR specialties were treated as separate silos. That is, recruiting was handled separately from performance management; training and development was still another discipline. Different persons were responsible, and information flow between functions was limited. Now, organizations are integrating the functions. They establish one set of goals for their talent functions (from selection through off-boarding), they communicate one message, and data flow logically from step to step.

2. Organizations are creating competency models. They, in turn, become the glue that holds together the different disciplines. The competency model used to select employees is the same one used to train, evaluate, and promote them.

3. Career and talent management have become more strategic in focus and outcomes. Career and talent management are recognized as a competitive advantage, not an employee benefit (and is recognized as one of the most effective ways to reduce turnover of valuable employees). In the past, career development might have meant taking a standardized test to determine whether you should be a cook, baker, or candlestick maker. Today, career development often means helping an employee to see the best opportunities for growth within the company. Having the right people at the right time and the right cost in the right positions has demonstrable impact on the organization.

Competency-based trainers need to be aware of these trends and consider the implications for training. For example, can the competency-based trainer work in closer partnership with other HR functions for the benefit of all parties? Can competency models be jointly developed, shared, and maintained? How can competency-based training be linked to organizational strategic objectives? For example, if maintaining key performers is critical, career development programs are often one of the best approaches to improve employee retention. Many times organization strategy implementation relies on the availability of certain skill sets, and here again the competency-based trainer can have a strategic, measurable impact.

Providing a viable career development program is likely to be labor-intensive and beyond the capability of one individual, so technology will most likely be required.

An *integrated talent management system* is the most likely choice to meet this need effectively and at reasonable cost. The details of these systems vary. Exhibit 5–1 gives an overview of one: the *Focus* Talent Management Suite developed by Business Decisions of Chicago, Illinois. The competency models created in the first module, competency modeling and job profiling, form the target or map for employee selection, training, assessment, and other areas. The second module, candidate and employee assessments, is used to assess people vis-à-vis one or multiple competency models. The third module, leader and employee development, is used to look at the gap between target competencies versus individual competence to create an individual development plan that addresses organizational priorities. The career planning module appears next, and it allows employees to find jobs within the organization that are good matches with their competencies (today or in the future) and their personal career preferences.

Exhibit 5–1: The *Focus* Talent Management Suite

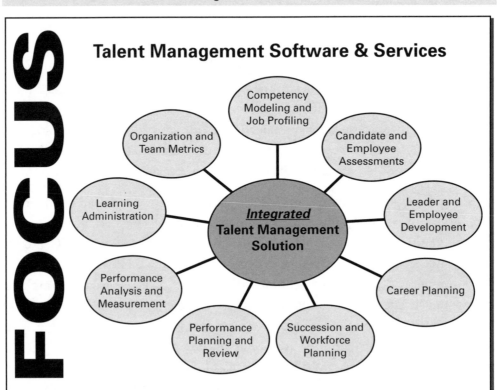

Coaching/Mentoring AOE

Competency-based trainers are very likely to find themselves cast into the role of development coach to employees seeking to develop themselves, or equally as likely to be required to support supervisors who have been placed in a coaching role. Additionally, given the growing importance of mentoring programs as an element of training, it may become their responsibility to design and implement a program to match mentors and mentees. Technology can do a lot to support these coaching and mentoring processes.

For coaching, Learning Management Systems (LMS) or Talent Management Systems (TMS) can provide the following services:

- ▶ assessments that can help identify development priorities for present or future roles; some have fairly sophisticated algorithms that consider the relative importance of different competencies, the desired performance level, and an employee's current readiness
- ▶ development resource libraries that suggest appropriate learning for competency-based development given individual development priorities and learning preferences
- ▶ individual development plans that document detailed development goals, action steps, and success measures; progress can be tracked and evaluated
- ▶ 360-multirater tools that provide feedback on development needs or progress from many perspectives, such as peers, subordinates, and internal or external customers.

For mentoring, LMS or TMS can facilitate the following services:

- ▶ individuals to register as mentors, select areas of expertise, provide personal profiles, and indicate current availability
- ▶ mentees' searches for mentors with particular competencies, characteristics (for example, male/female), and demographics (for example, location or division)
- ▶ the acceptance and contracting process between mentors and mentees
- ▶ tracking and reporting on mentee progress and program effectiveness
- ▶ evaluating mentors
- ▶ documenting who has mentored and who has been mentored.

Reliance Industries Ltd. is a case in point. This company has developed blended coaching and mentoring programs intended to quickly transfer existing knowledge to new employees. These include

- knowledge, skills, and abilities (KSAs) defined for mentors and mentees
- mentors trained in a mentoring workshop—their training style is assessed, and this is mapped to the learning styles of potential protégés
- a detailed syllabus based on the KSA matrix required of the mentee
- lesson plans (modules) defined
- lesson plans uploaded on a mentoring portal
- daily diary for mentors and mentees
- online tracking of the progress of learning, certification and validation— validation and certification are based on written test as well as interviews
- monetary rewards for both mentors and mentees after successful, accelerated completion of learning modules and certification.

Delivering Training AOE

Data from ASTD's *2009 State of the Industry Report* verify that organizations are using technology more than ever before to deliver learning and that the use of instructor-led learning has diminished. Discrete learning events in traditional classroom settings are gradually shifting to learning experiences that occur at the workstation and at the worker's pace.

Trainers are blessed with many technologically savvy alternatives for delivering competency-based training (see Rothwell, Butler, Maldonado, Hunt, Peters, Li, & Stern, 2006). New approaches such as podcasts, social networking, wikis, blogs, and web conferences have proven effective for delivering content quickly and at lesser expense than traditional classroom-based approaches. Many of these technologies are accessible to even the smallest organizations or organizations lacking the most resources.

Web conferences are a perfect example of an inexpensive, easily implemented technology that will pay for itself almost immediately. Organizations can cut travel costs and time associated with classroom learning. The services are hosted externally, so little is needed to use them other than a computer and internet connection. The cost to use web meeting software has dropped dramatically (following the typical trend of most technology) and a number of free web conferencing alternatives now exist.

How do the new learning delivery methodologies differ from traditional classroom training? Many of the differences are similar to those that distance and e-learning introduced some years ago. First, they utilize multimedia, which can be more effective at conveying some concepts ("a picture is worth a thousand words"); reach people with varying learning styles; and can be more engaging. Second, they feature interactive, two-way communication that helps learners retain information and enjoy the training process. Third, they are more modular and therefore more personalized, allowing learners to proceed at their own best pace and access the learning just in time when their motivation levels to learn are highest.

Examples abound. We mention a few:

▶ Merrill Lynch launched the GoLearn program to deliver training via BlackBerry. They compared mandated courses offered both at Merrill Lynch University and GoLearn and found that the learning results were equal. However, the GoLearn training required 30 to 45 percent less time and had a 12 percent higher completion rate. All of the participants indicated that they would like to see more training in that format. (Brown, 2009)

▶ Tyco/Grinnell has built a prototype that allows mobile phone access to customer data and orders (the information is read over the telephone), access to "Books on Tape," the capability to record individual messages/tips for group access, and access to recent messages from the CEO. (Metcalf, 2008)

▶ Epocrates, Inc., provides 15-minute courses and decision support to health care professionals via iPhones, BlackBerrys, Palms, and Windows Mobile devices. The intent is to provide healthcare professionals with an information source that is quickly and easily accessible as well as reliable. The company states that more than 900,000 healthcare professionals, including one in three U.S. physicians, use Epocrates' mobile and web-based products to help them reduce medical errors, improve patient care, and increase productivity. (Epocrates, 2009)

Part of the new reality is that learning does not always come from experts (Johnson, 2008). Collaborative learning empowers all participants with an opportunity to add to the body of knowledge based on their experiences. Competency-based trainers may play a vital role in maintaining the integrity of content being distributed through monitoring and getting the assistance of experts to verify information.

Technology-based learning is more than hardware and software. Competency-based trainers will be at the forefront of creating a new mindset that encourages people to learn constantly, even in informal settings, when stationary or on the go. It changes the face of training from knowledge presentation to knowledge distribution. It enables access at the moment of need and reduces the necessity for a learner to memorize information.

Designing Learning AOE

As organizations evolve their learning design or content development to meet a variety of needs such as increasing volume, lower costs, and on-demand learning, more technology is required. The use of technology for learning delivery may be more obvious than its use for learning content, but the use is equivalent, and in fact design and delivery often go together. That is, new delivery mechanisms are typically needed to utilize new content development techniques.

A *Learning Content Management System* (LCMS) is typically used for learning design. They may be integrated or separate from an LMS. Given business imperatives to develop and deliver content more rapidly, LCMs are evolving from tools for creating e-learning to tools for designing knowledge resources that can be flexibly re-used for a number of different learning needs. These systems are less prevalent than LMS systems (12 to 13 percent market penetration; Mallon et al., 2009). However, we can expect LCMSs to become more mainstream quickly both because of the move to a greater emphasis on informal learning and the business advantages associated with effective management and distribution of information to employees.

Bersin and Associates (Howard, 2007) have developed a Learning Content Maturity Model that is a framework for how organizations evolve in learning content design and management (see Exhibit 5–2). A mature learning organization can at different times operate at any of the five levels, and none of the levels is inherently bad. However, the higher an organization advances on the hierarchy, the more capacity it has to develop content, particularly content designed to be accessible 24/7 and to meet individual needs. Each level inherently involves more technology.

The Bersin stages of learning maturity are as follows:

1. *Traditional:* This was the best practice, prevalent approach of producing learning content prior to the advent of e-learning. The training is an instructor-led course. Content is built with the assistance of SMEs using

Exhibit 5–2: Bersin & Associates Learning Content Maturity Model

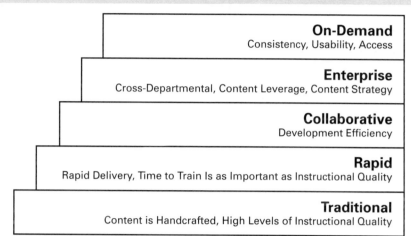

On-Demand
Consistency, Usability, Access

Enterprise
Cross-Departmental, Content Leverage, Content Strategy

Collaborative
Development Efficiency

Rapid
Rapid Delivery, Time to Train Is as Important as Instructional Quality

Traditional
Content is Handcrafted, High Levels of Instructional Quality

Source: Bersin & Associates: The Learning Maturity Model: Developing a Framework for Integrated Training and Knowledge Management, 2007.

traditional instructional design methodology (that is, "ADDIE"— Analyze, Design, Develop, Implement, Evaluate). Technology is used for content authoring and publishing, such as desktop publishing software. Self-paced CD-ROMS or other similar media may also be used. The approach may still be the method of choice in certain circumstances, such as when there is plenty of time for development, where there are many learners that can benefit, where the content does not change quickly, and where high production quality is justified.

2. *Rapid:* Rapid development, as the name implies, responds to the need to get learning content out the door quickly without compromising quality. Lack of development resources may also be a driver. Time to develop learning might go from several months to a few weeks, and costs savings of 50 percent or greater are achievable. This can be achieved through greater process efficiencies (for example, using templates to empower SMEs to build sound content) and technology (for example, tools for rapid authoring in common content presentation formats such as PowerPoint).

3. *Collaborative:* Collaborative development further increases capacity and scope of content development. It is driven by needs for greater content variety, more frequent updating, and multiple or multinational

workforces. To meet these needs, content development becomes dispersed geographically and more specialized, which in turn requires improved project management. Standards for content are developed and enforced.

Technology becomes even more critical at this stage. It helps integrate multiple authoring tools or provides the flexibility needed by diverse staff. It allows multiple persons to work on development without overwriting the work of others through check-in/check-out version control or other file management approaches. Web-based collaborative workspaces such as SharePoint may be utilized. The same technologies allow for increasing use of resources external to the organization. Finally, page-based development is common at this level, which allows for an early stage of content reuse.

4. *Enterprise:* Content development capacities are expanded further. This is driven by a desire to personalize content and be less course-centric, to work better across departments, to incorporate still more content sources and types into learning, to increase recycling of content, as well as to continue to increase volume. Content development practices are similar to those used at the collaborative level, but content is handled, deployed, and leveraged differently.

   Raw content ("learning objects") is separated from its delivery mechanism, so that the content can be reused and delivered by many different mechanisms or channels and can be dynamically assembled in unique combinations, allowing personalization. Technology tools are capable of fast and flexible assembly of content that has been tagged and stored in content repositories. An LMS can also be used to deliver the right training (or other planned learning experiences) to the right person, depending on roles, certifications, and compliance requirements.

5. *On-Demand:* At this highest level of evolution (to date), we bring personalized learning content to the learner at the time and point of need in the workplace. This is just-in-time training. With on-demand training, we put learning into the hands of individuals and empower

employees to learn while they are doing (instead of having to learn first). In addition, learning can be contextualized (specific to the task at hand). At this level, the training evolves from learning to on-the-job performance support and knowledge sharing. Training can become better aligned with strategic organization objectives and desired business results.

Learning is integrated with other enterprise systems outside the realm of the traditional training department, such as performance and talent management or knowledge management systems, putting whatever the employee needs at his fingertips. For example, learning material related to the steps of the performance management process, such as writing SMART goals (Table 5–1) or giving an effective performance review, could be integrated appropriately within the workflow of the performance management process. Or, a sales representative might have product information, client information, and proposal and pricing information integrated into one user-friendly system with individual learning objects easily accessible. Trainers have the opportunity to correlate sale-results data with data on which individuals have completed what training, and to better understand how learning is or is not contributing to performance.

Table 5–1. Characteristics of SMART Objectives

	Description
Specific	Objectives must represent the specific desired outcomes from the standpoint of al critical stakeholders.
Measurable	Objectives must be developed so that measures of success are evident. Measurable indicators make it possible to assess whether the objectives are achieved or not. The objective must also be such that the program owners can actually take the measure, given the type of measure as well as resource constraints.
Achievable	Objectives must stretch participants, designers, and developers, toward improvement but remain within 'arm's lenghth.'
Realistic	Objectives must be realistic given the conditions, resources, time period, and support available to achieve the objectives.
Time bound	Objectives must represent the achievement of results within a certain period of time.

Note: For variations of SMART, visit http://rapidbi.com/created/WriteSMARTobjectives.html

In summary, as your organization progresses in capacity and sophistication to design training, technology will be increasingly important. Given that demand for competency training may outstrip the capacity to provide it, technology-enhanced learning design can be a great boon for competency-based trainers.

Managing the Learning Function AOE

The practice of using technology to manage the learning function has been in place in many organizations for more than a decade and can be a boon to the competency-based trainer. Bersin and Associates (Mallon et al., 2009) report that overall, 40 percent of U.S. organizations have an LMS and 80 percent of large organizations have them in place.

Relatively standard, basic features (to name a few) of an LMS include

- describing available training and learning resources through training calendars or links to organization competencies
- managing registration, prerequisites, nomination, and approval for a training activity
- managing class rosters, including waiting lists
- communicating and reminding employees about a variety of topics, such as schedules, pre-work, and other requirements
- launching e-learning
- evaluating trainees
- evaluating instructors and training
- tracking attendance
- preparing certificates of training completion
- managing and tracking instructors
- managing certification and compliance programs
- storing and retrieving individual training records
- analyzing and reporting
- interfacing with other corporate HR systems.

Since 2000, most LMSs have evolved into a portal that allows users to manage administrative aspects of their own learning and launch e-learning. Another trend is to use the systems to manage business partner training and to promote training to customers. Currently, the systems are evolving to support social/collaborative learning and to manage learning content through knowledge management.

Managing Organizational Knowledge AOE

Knowledge management (KM) is the process of identifying useful knowledge and making it readily available to others when they need it. Most KM systems are by necessity dynamic: Participants continually share, enhance, and maintain information, thereby supporting continuous performance improvement. Other benefits of KM may include improved productivity enhancement, cost reduction, as well as innovation and growth. That said, many KM programs have been plagued with obstacles and costly setbacks (Davenport, 2005; Hall, 2009).

KM extends learning to the work environment, and as a competency-based trainer, you may find yourself providing advice or even "owning" these systems. At a minimum, you will likely be responsible for helping users understand and use the benefits of a KM system, as well as how to personally contribute. Then, you may need to provide ongoing encouragement and reinforcement.

Knowledge can be explicit such as company processes, practices, and standards, or tacit which is the knowledge and experience that resides in the minds of people that do the work. Impending baby boomer retirements in virtually all industries raise the importance of capturing tacit information now. The often stated mantra for developing KM systems is "people, process, and technology." People are clearly needed to sponsor the process, and to share, reformulate, validate, and update knowledge. Processes are needed for all of the steps that people are performing. Finally, some type of intuitive, user-friendly knowledge portal technology is required for capturing, distributing just in time, maintaining, and improving the knowledge.

Given that some kind of electronic tool will be used for KM, a choice must be made between settling for current tools in hand or acquiring technology designed for KM. Sophisticated KM technology can provide a variety of capabilities. For example:

- Sophisticated database search capabilities, including
  - Filtering of responses for searches that are too narrow or too broad
  - Use of question-and-answer dialogues to help users navigate to an answer more quickly
  - Personalized response that provides exact answers to specific questions
  - Coaching users on how to improve their search
- Information managers that provide
  - Work flow for content authoring, editing, review, and publishing
  - Capabilities to connect to existing databases so that data don't need to be transformed and placed into one, centralized knowledge base

   ▶ Analytics that allow
- Identification of gaps in content
- Analysis of key information support needs

Regardless of the technology decision made, consider the basic steps for implementing KM (Atwood, 2009):

1. Determine needs for information and ways of accessing information
2. Locate information sources
3. Choose information gathering systems
4. Compile, confirm, and distribute knowledge
5. Maintain knowledge.

The basic steps appear to be simple enough, but managers of KM systems face significant challenges. For example, information could be out-of-date in 30 days or less, but it isn't simple to cull out information that is no longer current or usable. Who monitors that only "useful" information is added? Who has the last say on what information, especially tacit knowledge, is valid? Who is responsible for ensuring that the latest information is entered into the system? What are the incentives for contributing information versus hoarding it for personal benefit? A significant investment is required to maintain a KM system. Many systems have been abandoned soon after determining that their return-on-investment was unclear or not equal to their costs.

Despite many failures, successful KM is within reach of most organizations if proper care is exercised in answering the people–processes–technology questions. Some systems are actually very simple, while others will only be suited to larger organizations. For example:

   ▶ A bank has identified about 400 specialty areas important for serving its customers. A learning professional facilitated the process of identifying two internal "go-to" experts for each topic. A directory was created with the expert names, email addresses, and telephone extensions. This system has proven to be both effective and highly rated by bank employees.

   ▶ A manufacturing company tries to spread the learning benefit by having employees that attend external training make presentations to peers that did not attend. An average of 30 to 40 employees attend each presentation. Each year, the company celebrates the anniversary of this program to promote knowledge sharing.

▶ A manufacturer has a KM system that includes both explicit and tacit information. Users can quickly find
- Standard Operating Procedures and Standard Operating Conditions
- Standard Maintenance Procedures
- Original Equipment Manufacturers' (OEM) documents, drawings, specifications, and Material Safety Data Sheets
- Failure Abnormality Reports and Reliability Issues
- Benchmarking Data
- Lessons Learned.

▶ Many customer support functions rely on KM systems to respond quickly, cost-effectively, and correctly to customers needing assistance, and most important, to increase customer satisfaction. Back-and-forth exchanges between customers and support are captured, but these databases gain additional value by inserting links to useful references and by re-authoring and indexing with keywords so that the content is more readily available and is designed for quick provision of solutions. Because the bulk of inquiries into a specific issue have been found to typically have a life cycle of 30 to 45 days (Hall, 2009), it is important to post new information very quickly when issues or new needs arise.

Common Mistakes in Selecting Technology and Vendors

When you make a technology purchase decision, you need to consider much more than gleaming new hardware or software. You also need to be certain that you are choosing a vendor that will provide you what you need over the course of what hopefully will be a long-term relationship. Selecting a technology and vendor is surprisingly similar to choosing a spouse (see Exhibit 5–3).

That faulty choices are prevalent is probably not news to anyone. Selections of spouses or technology can be quite complex. What are the common mistakes you should consciously avoid to prevent a poor technology acquisition decision?

▶ *Evaluating vendors before you know your requirements.* This approach can result in relying on gut reactions or focusing on the wrong decision criteria, and at that point you are like a gambler relying on his good luck. Like the gambler, you may "go bust."

Exhibit 5–3: Choice of a Spouse—or a Technology Vendor

1. There is a large element of chance. There are far too many potential choices to consider all of them. You will only consider a small percentage of the candidates.

2. There is more than one right choice—and more than one with which you could be happy.

3. You can be overly influenced by superficial features.

4. The quality of the decision you make is not necessarily improved by whether you spend a little or a lot of time evaluating the candidates.

5. If you aren't focusing on the most important decision criteria, you may be vulnerable to making mistakes.

6. There is a "honeymoon" period. For technology, and marriage, it often occurs before the wedding (or the technology implementation)! No choice is perfect. Attaining and maintaining happiness will require effort.

7. Break-ups are messy, yet unfortunately, all too common! You typically will have invested a lot of time and money. Breaking the relationship is likely to cause recriminations, inconvenience, some temporary disorientation, and costs.

8. You may or may not be wiser the next time you choose.

Although this may seem so basic that a warning is not necessary, it is easy to give too much consideration to the likeability of a salesperson or his or her speaking skills. Gorgeous PowerPoint® slides (or presenters) too often distract evaluators from the relative merit of a solution. You need a well-defined, prioritized set of requirements to make a good decision.

Another trap related to lack of criteria is becoming enamored with features vendors hype that add little value or possibly detract from the solution. For example, if your supervisors are evaluating their direct reports on accomplishment of development goals, do you really benefit from a "writing assistant," a feature that will allow supervisors to insert generic comments (developed by a software vendor) instead of their own? Granted, not every supervisor writes well, but aren't we defeating the purpose of feedback by giving supervisors an alternative to providing their own customized comments?

Knowledgeable vendors can be very helpful in educating you. They may even have technical sales staff that will help you decide what you really need. Furthermore, knowing that it takes a lot of time and effort to assemble a list of requirements and having a vendor provide you with a list could help you create yours. You will probably be given a list of requirements that jibes remarkably closely with their offering, but compiling suggested lists of requirements from several strong vendors (as well as from reputable industry analysts) can lessen the time and effort to assemble requirements and may help you identify important requirements that otherwise could have been overlooked.

> ▶ *Being mislead by a written proposal.* Vendor proposals provide essential information, but you may err in how you evaluate proposals or by eliminating a vendor based solely on proposal responses.

To maximize the value of vendor proposals, you will want to define what you are looking for by writing a Request for Proposal (RFP). The RFP usually contains your list of requirements as well as other important evaluation criteria (such as similar experience and references) to which prospective vendors must respond.

You are looking for vendors that can supply your requirements, hopefully "out-of-the-box" rather than needing to develop new functionality. That said, requirements can be a bit ambiguous, and it is not unknown for some vendors to indicate that they have everything! To reduce the tendency for vendors to overpromise, you can ask vendors to briefly describe how they meet each requirement.

Besides the "bells and whistles" that the vendor can offer, a proposal can give you other valuable insights such as how much that vendor might value your business, their attention to detail, and professionalism. You are right to be concerned when a proposal doesn't clearly address the issues in your RFP, when it is loaded with extraneous material and appendices, or when you see the name of another potential client in the proposal a vendor has submitted to you! Realistically, most vendors will use "boilerplate" (material they place in every proposal), but they should clearly demonstrate that they care about your specific needs by addressing your specific concerns.

On the other hand, a "light" proposal does not always indicate bad technology. It is possible for a company to be better at developing and implementing a technology than it is at writing proposals. Furthermore, just because a vendor's proposal includes magnificent graphics or it weighs 10 kilos doesn't necessarily mean that you will be satisfied with that vendor. In fact, a lengthy proposal padded with endless appendices may be more of an indicator of high cost than of quality.

> ▶ *Lack of stakeholder input.* This error occurs when you exclude other business stakeholders such as end users, procurement, or IT from participating meaningfully in the evaluation. A variety of perspectives are required to make a good decision.

One of the secrets of the vendor selection process is utilizing the right combination of experts and end users. Evaluation of a dentist is an apt analogy. Even for something as seemingly straightforward as teeth cleaning, it takes an expert to accurately evaluate quality. Meanwhile, the patient has a valid and important evaluation of how the process was for them, but it would be inappropriate to judge a dentist solely on his or her pleasantness. Similarly, evaluating learning technology may require a combination of learning expertise, information technology, as well as end user experience. Giving too much weight to any of the three perspectives may lead you astray.

> ▶ *Vendor favoritism.* This manifests itself as a strong preference or even the selection of the winning vendor before the evaluation process has begun (sometimes referred to as a "wired" selection process). Most often, the favoritism is based on past relationships. Although the vendor might be competent, there are other vendors that deserve legitimate consideration.

Examples are legion of wired vendor selections. Strict rules of impartiality may help a bit (such as sharing questions and answers from one prospective vendor with all other vendors), but often these rules do more to create a perception of impartiality than to prevent vendor favoritism. An unfortunate by-product of vendor favoritism is that other viable vendors may sense that they don't have a legitimate opportunity to win the business and they may invest only a small amount in their proposal or may not participate at all in the process. This creates a self-fulfilling prophecy in that the favored vendor looks best.

Besides the necessity of maintaining an open competition and an open mind on each vendor prospect, it is important that you assure prospective vendors the best you can that you will give real consideration to their offering and that the evaluation process is fair and impartial.

Getting It Done

In this chapter, you learned about new technologies you can leverage for competency-based training and how technology can support many of the learning and performance professional's areas of expertise.

How do you believe that technology (combined with good learning practices) can be used to improve the process of competency-based training? Make a list.

Communicating About Competency-Based Approaches

What's Inside This Chapter

In this chapter, you'll learn

▶ How to define "communicating about competency-based approaches"

▶ The importance of communicating about competency-based approaches

▶ How to communicate about competency-based approaches before and during competency identification and on a continuing basis.

Communicating about competency-based approaches means more than just "informing." It means demonstrating the value of competency-based approaches in a compelling way at the outset of the effort. It means talking to others on a continuous basis and mounting a communication strategy to support the effort. Bringing about change requires continuing communication.

Introducing competency-based approaches in an organization (whether as the competency developer or the learning professional charged with implementing a set of competencies into training programs) is a major culture change effort, and it requires sustained commitment.

Basic Rule 1

It is not enough for management to give one briefing on a new competency system and expect everyone to buy-in and accept it. Most failures in implementing competency implementation stem from poor communication efforts.

Generally, you will want to develop sponsors for competency-based training. These are enthusiastic proponents who champion the concept and process and provide credibility. You will also want to court the support of a variety of stakeholders: the people who are affected and could derail the process if they are not supportive. In addition to explaining the technical details of identifying, assessing, and developing competencies, the competency-based professional must explain and sell the benefits to sponsors and stakeholders in order to win their support. If people can see that a competency-based approach helps them meet some of their accountabilities, improves profitability, or reduces costs, building support will be much simpler. For example, many potential sponsors will be enthusiastic about developing talent from within versus relying on costly and time-consuming external recruitment. Communications must continue even after the initial approval of sponsors. It is important to regularly communicate about the objectives and business reasons justifying competency-based training and tout the continuing results obtained from it.

Building Your Communication Plan

Before embarking on competency-based training, practitioners should complete six key steps outlined in Exhibit 6–1. A worksheet intended to help organize your thinking is presented as a tool in Exhibit 6–2 as well.

In addition to this six-step model, another option (and the two are not mutually exclusive) is to create a steering committee or advisory group to guide your efforts. One of the best ways to build support and communicate with key stakeholders is to

Exhibit 6–1: Building Your Communication Plan

Step 1: Identifying the key stakeholders
Step 2: Targeting change objectives for each stakeholder group at each project
Step 3: Pinpointing special concerns of each stakeholder group and dealing with resistance
Step 4: Crafting a stream of messages and channels tied to the technical work plan
Step 5: Implementing the plan
Step 6: Evaluating the effectiveness of communication methods

involve them. A steering committee can also provide valuable ideas on how to keep the project on track, and its members will have access to frank feedback from their constituents. They, in effect, serve as an advanced warning system for potential or developing problems.

Step 1: Identifying the Key Stakeholders

Start any change effort, including the introduction of competency-based learning, by identifying the key stakeholders. These are the people who will influence the effort and will be affected by it. Realize that different stakeholders care about different issues. The "what's in it for me" will differ, depending on the stakeholder. For example:

- ▶ Top managers will often find appealing that competency-based approaches address increasing productivity and building bench strength.
- ▶ Middle and front-line managers will find appealing that competency-based approaches may make it easier to find the right people when they are needed to fill vacancies.
- ▶ Individual contributors may find appealing that competencies will make more transparent what is required for job success and promotional opportunities.
- ▶ Labor leaders may find appealing that competencies will make job progression more objective and less prone to supervisors favoring some individuals over others.

Don't forget to include other groups that may help in the implementation. For example, you might want to invite legal, IT, or corporate communications to participate.

Step 2: Targeting Change Objectives for Each Stakeholder Group at Each Project

Try to clarify what different stakeholders want from a competency-based learning effort. What would they most like to see? Here are some of the questions you may want to ask:

▶ What will be a successful outcome to you of this project?
▶ What are the organizational strengths that will contribute to the success of this project?
▶ What are the organizational barriers, and how can we overcome them?
▶ What competency-based training methods will work well within our organization and culture?
▶ What is the most effective way to communicate throughout the organization?
▶ What role would you recommend you play in this project?
▶ Who would you recommend for the subject matter expert teams?
▶ What competencies are most important in your area?
▶ Do you feel that we should test for competency acquisition?

You will also want to determine how to measure the accomplishment of stakeholder objectives and perhaps how to tie them to the organization's strategic objectives and business needs. Measurement is an area where you can consider incorporating Kirkpatrick's four levels of evaluation. What attitudes or opinions need to change? What skills? What on-the-job behavior? What business results?

Step 3: Pinpointing Special Concerns of Each Stakeholder Group and Dealing With Resistance

As previously stated, you should ask stakeholders to help identify organizational barriers and how to overcome them. Some individuals and groups may resist competency-based learning. For example, competency-based learning may entail a heightened level of individual accountability, both during the learning process and for the ultimate results of that learning. Individuals that have grown up in environments where most training was presented in a traditional classroom may resist new learning for-

Worksheet 6–2: A Worksheet for Organizing Communication

Directions: Use this worksheet to organize your thinking about how to communicate before undertaking a competency modeling. For each question posed in the left column below, answer it in the right column. You may wish to use this worksheet in staff meetings to involve others in planning for communication about competencies.

Questions	Answers
How will you and the organization . . .	
1. Identify the key stakeholders who should be informed about the effort (such as members of the target group, their immediate supervisors, HR practitioners not otherwise involved in the effort, and top managers who may have to authorize and support action)?	
2. Target change objectives for each stakeholder group at each step of the competency project?	
3. Pinpoint any special concerns of each stakeholder group (realizing that they may differ in what they want out of it) and make sure that messages at each step will address those concerns?	
4. Craft a stream of messages and channels (modes of communication) tied step by step to the technical work plan of identifying, assessing, and using competencies?	
5. Implement the plan, using a combination of channels (such as individual, group, and organizational) and methods, realizing that one approach to getting information out will rarely be adequate to build and sustain ownership?	
6. Establish methods of evaluating the effectiveness of communication methods before, during, and after the introduction of competency-based training and competency-based learning?	

mats such as e-learning as well as their increased responsibility to identify appropriate development resources for themselves based on their greatest development needs.

Another common source of resistance comes from anxiety about any sort of testing for competence. Employees wonder about the potential consequences if they don't perform well. Older employees may be particularly anxious because they may not have been assessed for many years, and they may lament this new accountability for competence, especially compared to a more traditional emphasis on experience and seniority. Even some in training roles may prefer the familiar status quo. It is important to anticipate as well as search out any and all concerns and facilitate solutions that can reduce or eliminate the barriers. When possible, involve any resistors in solving the problems and try to engage them as on-going steering committee members or advisors.

Positioning initial efforts as a pilot study is a good tactic that can blunt criticism and make it easier to address concerns. A pilot study implies that you are testing out your processes and that you will be evaluating what works well, what doesn't work well, and that you will be making adjustments. It is a clear acknowledgment that you "don't know what you don't know," that glitches are a likely possibility, but that continuous improvement is the intention. Another positive by-product of a pilot is that you can create experienced, influential reference groups that can communicate and champion the process, sometimes more credibly than you can.

Step 4: Crafting a Stream of Messages and Channels Tied to the Technical Work Plan

The *technical work plan* is the process used to identify competencies and behavioral indicators, assess individuals against them, identify performance and development gaps, and narrow or close the gaps through individual development efforts. The *communication plan* is the process of explaining and building support for the change effort—that is, competency-based learning—before, during, and after each step of the technical work plan.

For each step in the technical work plan, a corresponding step (or series of steps) should be taken to explain what is happening, why it is worth doing, and what results are expected. These steps are intended to produce a stream of continuing communication to key stakeholders to keep them apprised of what is happening and what they are getting out of it. Frequently we see a fine job done with initial communications, but that is often followed by few or no further updates. As a rough rule of thumb, we recommend contacting key constituencies (hopefully with news of positive results) every 90 to 100 days.

Logistics—Who, When, and What

Each step of the communication plan should clarify who will do what. Who will initiate messages? Approve them? When should those messages be transmitted, through what method, to whom, and with what desired results?

A poor communication plan will usually mean that the grapevine moves faster than the messages coming from the right people. The grapevine moves along friendship channels and zeroes in on what people may fear or find worrisome. A well-orchestrated communication plan will make it possible for people to get official messages as fast as what travels on the grapevine. For that reason, it is often worthwhile to consider establishing anonymous call-in lines or message boards in which management commits to an answer to any question posed within 24 hours. That will provide an avenue for people to get the right information rather than live in terror of the rumors they hear. It will also require radar—or an early warning system—to try to anticipate concerns that may surface and address them before they do. A diverse steering committee can alert you to "the word on the street."

An effective communication strategy goes beyond simply communicating by mass media, such as websites or "town hall meetings." Although those are important, they are not enough. Those who launch a competency-based learning effort will need to consider

- ▶ individual communication such as personal selling and one-on-one meetings with managers or workers
- ▶ group communication such as an HR representative visiting each department to discuss the competency-based learning initiative
- ▶ mass communication such as online videos that describe what competency-based learning is and how people will benefit from it
- ▶ integrated communication that is embedded in existing communication that goes out from the organization such as the employee handbook, on-boarding program, organizationally sponsored training, to ensure that information is provided about competency-based learning.

Step 5: Implementing the Plan

Good communication is not a one-shot effort. It requires sustained effort. Without a continuous communication program, a variety of negative consequences are possible. Key stakeholders may be alarmed or annoyed if wholesale changes or fine-tuning occur to existing processes and their views were not solicited and carefully considered. Other people who are less involved may lose awareness of competency-based learning and dismiss it as "just another flavor of the month." Still others could start to believe rumors that may surface about it. In time, that will destroy the effort and people will fall back into old routines that are comfortable and familiar. For this reason, communication must be ongoing. Integrated communication is particularly important for that purpose. Every official channel and message should be reviewed to see if appropriate messages about competency-based learning are embedded. Look for some way to bring up the topic at management meetings and review why the effort was launched, review what has happened with the effort, and demonstrate what results have been obtained from it for the organization and for each stakeholder group.

Step 6: Evaluating the Effectiveness of Communication Methods

How can the effectiveness of the communication effort be evaluated? There are several ways, of course. If you have created a steering or advisory committee, its members can provide informal but very useful information on how the program is being perceived in various departments and locations. Similarly, those most involved in implementing the process (for example, others in training, organization development and effectiveness, HR, and so on) may be interviewed and will be able to speak to the questions and stakeholder interactions they are having. Brief opinion surveys and focus groups can be used. You may even have a rating system in place that allows stakeholders to rate the program and communications (such as 1 through 5 stars) and to provide open-ended comments.

When using any or all of these data collection approaches, you can measure current reactions to your competency-based training program as well as reactions to your communication vehicles.

Communicating During the Competency-Based Learning Effort

Implementing competency-based learning requires successful execution. The six steps identified must be executed systematically. The most common mistake made is to assume that a one-shot communication effort at the beginning is all that is necessary; that is simply not effective.

For each competency identification project, learning professionals should ensure that there are kickoff meetings held with the targeted group(s) and their immediate supervisors to explain the project, detail how the results will be used, and explain why the effort is important to the organization. Individual meetings may need to be held with vocal critics to identify their concerns and answer their questions. When individuals are assessed against competency models, learning professionals need to ensure that each person is briefed about the effort beforehand, counseled about the results afterward, and is confident about how to pinpoint performance and development needs that should be the focus of individual development plans. Senior managers should periodically hold meetings to examine the progress made in developing high potentials—those who are both promotable and who are doing at least acceptable work in their present jobs.

At each step, stakeholders should be reminded of why the organization has committed to competency models, how they are related to strategic business objectives, and what results are being obtained. Without continuous tracking and ongoing communication, it is easy for stakeholders to forget about the effort and lose their commitment to it. Use the activity in Exhibit 6–3 to organize your thinking about how to brainstorm on these issues.

Exhibit 6–3: Keeping Attention on Competency-Based Training

Directions: Use this worksheet to structure your brainstorming on ways to keep attention on competency-based training and learning. For each question posed in the left column below, answer it in the right column. You may wish to use this Worksheet in staff meetings to involve others in planning for continuous communication.

Questions	Answers
How should the organization be kept apprised of the continuing competency-based training/learning effort? Consider:	
1. Who is the focus of competency-building efforts?	
2. What is being done?	
3. When are results being obtained?	
4. Where are results being obtained?	
5. Why are the results worthy of attention?	
6. How is the organization building competencies on a continuing basis?	

Getting It Done

You learned about the importance of communication to introduce and sustain competency-based approaches to training and learning. It is essential to keep reminding stakeholders why competency-based training and learning are being used, what results are being obtained from them, and why the organization should continue to use them. Most competency-based efforts fail not because the competency work is done poorly but because HR or learning and performance professionals forget to keep communicating about it to stakeholders. What do you think about that statement? Explain your thinking.

1. You have been asked to develop a briefing for managers on how to communicate with their staff about competencies. Prepare an outline for that briefing.
2. Prepare an outline of a training program on competencies for workers at all levels of the organization. Indicate what major topics will be addressed.
3. Prepare a project plan to show how information will be communicated about competencies on an annual basis after the competency-based effort has been launched. What topics should be discussed? What results should be described?

Using Competencies to Guide Learning—An Application Guide

What's Inside This Chapter

In this chapter, you'll learn

▶ How to use a competency model developed by someone else to guide the organization's training and development efforts
▶ How to reframe existing training so that it matches up to competency models.

Workplace learning professionals are likely to face two competency implementation scenarios. In one scenario, you are handed a complete model developed by someone else—a consulting firm, corporate headquarters, or the HR department—and asked to use it to guide the organization's future learning efforts. This scenario can mean establishing new courses or planning other developmental experiences where none previously existed.

In the other scenario, you are asked to relate an existing slate of online and on-site courses and other planned learning experiences to your organization's competencies and make available access to a DRG so that individuals and their immediate supervisors may find development activities relevant to specific competency gaps when preparing IDPs. Of course, many learning and performance professionals may be tasked to do both.

This chapter focuses on the "how to" of competency-based learning, offering guidance to learning and performance professionals on what to do and how to do it. It examines both scenarios described above.

Using Competency Models to Guide Training and Development Efforts

There is more than one right way to use competency models to guide training and development efforts. A common approach, however, is to begin with the competencies and the behavioral indicators linked to them, assuming they have been provided by another source. Learning and performance professionals who have had no involvement in the development of the competency models may wish to ask some tough questions about just how those competencies were developed.

Evaluating Existing Resources

It is necessary to evaluate what development resources (including training media as well as staff) are available and how they may be leveraged to meet specific competency learning needs of the organization.

We recommend that you take a very broad view of the potential development resources at your disposal to help employees. Resources consist of any material from any source that would help people build their competencies. These are some examples:

- articles or books
- videos and DVDs
- audiotapes and podcasts
- internal training courses
- external training courses
- conferences
- websites
- people inside the organization who may be especially good at demonstrating the appropriate behaviors

▷ communities of practice or interest groups that can provide helpful input

▷ knowledge management efforts and resultant databases

▷ work assignments inside the organization that may be especially good at building competency

▷ electronic performance support systems that provide guidance

▷ coaching or mentoring programs.

If development resources do not exist for critical competencies, or if resources exist but they have not been linked to competencies in your competency library, then some research will be required. Some organizations hire external contractors to do this work, since it can be time-consuming.

Linking competencies and their behaviors to the resources needed to build those competencies and elicit those behaviors is not an exact science. Keep in mind that you will gain additional value by categorizing the appropriateness of developmental resources for different levels of competency. In other words, some resources may be good for beginners, while others are more appropriate for experts. For example, if "negotiation skill" is the competency to be built, you may do a search of popular articles and books available from proven sources. Articles from the *Harvard Business Review* or the *Wall Street Journal*, or various books may be acceptable, but you must screen them for relevancy and appropriateness. Try to determine how advanced each resource is and if possible provide resources for all levels of competence; however, a few select, first-rate resources are better than many resources of unknown quality.

Think About This

How would you identify relevant, appropriate resources to list for a given competency, behavioral indicator, or a work output of a competency?

Linking Competency Resources and Behavior Indicators for Successful Outcomes

Searching for resources that will tie specifically to the behavioral indicators linked to each competency may be more fruitful than linking to the general competency description. The behavioral descriptions are more likely to clearly define what effective performers do and therefore what others can do to perform the competency effectively. The behavioral indicators will add focus to what is really important, plus help you avoid wasting time on development that won't have much impact.

Suppose, for instance, that the competency is "Customer Focus," one behavioral indicator linked to that competency might be something like "establishes methods of securing customers' feedback about their satisfaction with the services provided by the organization." The development resources identified should then be geared to helping learners demonstrate this and other specific behavioral indicators.

Training that is designed and delivered inside the organization, or custom made by vendors, is probably better able to elicit the specific behavioral indicators linked to the competency than resources taken from more general sources such as training course databases or general books or articles. This is particularly true, however, if the behavioral indicators have been specifically used in designing and developing the training.

Suppose, for instance, that the organization's learning and performance staff is tasked to develop a course for middle managers to build competencies for "Customer Focus." Typically, four to six behavioral indicators will be established, or more if different indicators are created for different levels (such as individual contributor, supervisor, and senior leader). Two behavioral indicators linked to the competency could be

- ▶ establishes methods of securing customers' feedback about their satisfaction with the services provided by the organization
- ▶ empathizes with customers, seeing service from their viewpoint.

If those are the behavioral indicators for the competency to be built by the course, then learning and performance professionals will need to establish instructional objectives, assessment methods, and follow-up activities to ensure that participants in the training can demonstrate and maintain these behaviors. For example, learning valid, practical methods of assessing customer feedback would likely be an instructional objective. Participants could be assessed using experiential activities, such as role playing, rather than completing paper-and-pencil tests of knowledge. In partnership with operating managers, they could be asked to do back-on-the-job assignments to facilitate transfer of learning from offsite training to on-the-job application.

Relating Existing Training to Competency Models

Another challenge that learning and performance professionals sometimes face is to relate existing training content such as a slate of existing online and on-site training courses to a competency library they have been handed by a third party (such as vendor, a corporate headquarters, or an HR department). This is different than the challenge described in the preceding section because it focuses on adapting training that already exists to a new competency framework.

To meet this challenge, we recommend the following practices:

Step 1. Prepare all training content with the following information and format to maximize its value for competency-based training and to facilitate users in making wise training choices:

▶ the general purpose of the development program: At a high level, what will participants be able to do as a result of the training, and how does that support the organization's mission or strategic goals? In short, why is it important?

▶ the instructional objectives: What competencies and behaviors will be covered?

▶ the outline of the development program

▶ the identity of the group for whom the training is targeted, including any prerequisites

▶ the method by which the training is delivered

▶ the method for evaluation of results.

Much of this information is available in existing course descriptions. Nevertheless, some information is often missing—for example, how the training relates to achieving the organization's mission or an organizational strategic objective. If complete information is not available for all training experiences, it will be necessary to update documentation to answer the questions posed above.

Step 2. Clearly relate existing training content to competencies and behaviors in the competency library and competency models. As noted above, it is important to identify what specific competencies and behaviors participants will be expected to demonstrate when they have finished the training program. The training should be rated twice on the same performance scale that will be used to evaluate or assess employees. The first rating states the prerequisite level of competence for taking the training, and the second rates the level at which the average individual will leave the training.

For example, a particular training resource on customer focus might be rated as a 1 as the prerequisite level of knowledge, and as a 2 on the average outcome at the end of the training. Something like the following training scale might be used:

1. *Beginner:* Rarely or never demonstrates the behaviors associated with this competency or demonstrates them with a low level of expertise.
2. *Novice:* Able to successfully apply this competency in relatively simple situations. Could further improve skills by increasing consistency and expertise.
3. *Skilled:* Demonstrates this competency at a high level of skill. Able to successfully demonstrate this competency in common situations. Could further improve by increasing expertise.
4. *Advanced:* Demonstrates this competency at a very high level of skill. Successfully applies this competency in situations requiring an advanced level of skill. Can assist others with the behaviors associated with this competency.
5. *Expert:* Able to successfully apply this competency in the most complex circumstances. Truly excellent in all elements of this competency. Serves as a role model for others. This person always performs at a very high level.

The scale can be made even more useful if behavioral examples specific to the training are used to better explain all five levels.

With these numerical ratings, it will be much easier for potential participants and their supervisors to evaluate the appropriateness of the training. Will the training take them to the level they need or at least get them started in that direction? Will it be over- or under-challenging? What is the relative merit of one training opportunity versus another? Given the time and cost associated to various training opportunities, it is even possible to gauge the relative return-on-investment.

Step 3. Relate the behaviors elicited by the existing training course identified in Step 2 to the behavioral indicators of the competency model applicable to the targeted group. Look for parallels. Also look for differences.

For example, suppose that the competency is "customer service skill" and a behavior in that model is to "smile at customers." If a training program is developed to build competence in customer service skill, it would therefore be necessary to ensure that learners are told about the importance of smiling at the customer. They may even be given role plays to practice smiling at customers with an observer counting how many times the learner does so.

Step 4. Make decisions about whether training content should be changed to better address competencies and behaviors. First, existing training resources can be evaluated and offerings can be strengthened with new content focused on important behaviors while more tangential information is eliminated. Second, new resources can be added to strengthen the range of offerings. It would be wise to concentrate on developing resources for competencies that are both widely used across the organization and critical to success. For example, organizations will want to identify plenty of resources for developing their core competencies, which are by definition required by all employees and critical to organizational success. In addition, there may be benefit to ensuring that resources are available for training across the whole spectrum of competence, from beginner to advanced. There is benefit to having a variety of training types available (such as classes, publications, and so on) to better meet individual learning preferences and styles as well as differing training situations such as for persons located at remote locations. Finally, it is important to consider the applicability of the training to the specific competency. For example, an individual who needs to strengthen his presentation skills may be best served by experiential training versus reading a book on the topic.

Putting it All Together—An Example

A simple example will help to clarify how this process can work. Suppose a company is offering a training program on "engaging employees." The purpose of the course is to teach supervisors, the targeted group, the basics of employee engagement and what they can do at their level to build an engaging climate for workers. The stated instructional objectives of the course are to ensure that, upon completion, participants will be able to:

- ▶ Define the term *engagement*.
- ▶ Describe three key actions that supervisors can take to build an engaging workplace climate.

Refer to Exhibit 7–1 for the course outline, based on instructional objectives.

Exhibit 7–1: Employee Engagement Course Outline

I. Introduction
- course purpose
- course objectives
- course outline and organization
- icebreaker
- debrief of the icebreaker

II. Defining engagement
- published definitions of *engagement*
- activity for participants to offer their own definitions of *engagement*
- debrief of the activity

III. Building an engaging workplace climate
- creating trust: say what you mean and mean what you say
- activity on creating trust
- debrief of the activity
- building self-confidence: give workers positive feedback on what they do
- activity on building self-confidence
- debrief of the activity
- asking for ideas to get workers interested by giving them chances to have a say in decisions
- activity on asking for ideas
- debrief of the activity

IV. Conclusion
- summary of the course
- identifying barriers that make it difficult to apply what was learned
- activity on "knocking down" the barriers
- planning for on-the-job application of the course principles

Note that the objectives, course content, and evaluation methods in Exhibit 7–1 are not obviously linked to any behaviors to elicit from participants other than the rather vague instructional objectives and the rather vague course outline. Placing the objectives, outline, and evaluation in this format, however, answers most of the key questions of Step 1.

To enact Step 2, move to the competency and behavioral level. What behaviors are elicited from participants in this training program? It would seem that they have at least some exposure to "creating trust," "building self-confidence," and "asking for ideas." But the specific behaviors they are taught to demonstrate are not very clear from the information provided. It may thus be necessary to examine the training material or sit in on a class and take notes on exactly how the participants are trained to behave.

Step 3 would now entail comparing the content of the training program with the behaviors it teaches in Exhibit 7–1. For example, we might determine that the prerequisite for taking the training should be that an individual is at least skilled (level 3 on a 5-point scale) in engaging employees, and we may judge that the average person will leave the training operating at an advanced level (level 4 on a 5-point scale). Furthermore, given the behaviors that are being taught, we might identify two, three, or more additional competencies that are also being taught in the training. For example, the training might also cover goal-setting and performance feedback. Thus, this training could be rated for multiple competencies.

As the final step advises, determine whether training content is acceptable, needs to be revised, or whether necessary development is best carried out using other development methods.

If the training is not teaching behaviors related to any competencies in the company competency library, or the competency has not been selected for any competency models, then it raises questions as to whether

▶ the competency model is incomplete; or
▶ the training program is not really necessary.

If the training is clearly related to critical competencies, you will still want to assess how well the training content elicits the behaviors linked to the competency and job success. If the answer is "effectively," then nothing further is needed. If the answer is "not very well," then the training program should be revised to ensure that it is aligned with the behavioral indicators found in the competency model.

Alternatively, the existing training may be related to important competencies and behaviors, but other training may be much better suited to current needs. For example, it might be that e-learning will be more attractive to participants and less costly to the organization than existing classroom training. Or, it could be that the existing three-day format is unpopular with participants and their supervisors because it takes them away from work for too long. Given the information you have on the most critical behaviors, you may be able to cut the training to a single day with very little loss of critical information. Participant evaluations will also provide guidance to important changes.

One final note: Learning and performance professionals should always consider whether participants have been assigned to appropriate learning experiences, and if so, to those that will provide the most value. Should all supervisors in Exhibit 7–1 be forced to attend training on engaging workers? Has some form of competency assessment been performed first so that only those needing to participate in the program are asked to attend? Even if all could benefit, is it possible that some could benefit more from training on different competencies, such as budgeting or project planning? If employee competency levels have not been assessed, how are learning and performance professionals sure that all participants really need the training?

A Case Study: Evaluating a Leadership Development Program

Introduction

Manitoba Lotteries Corporation (MLC), a Crown Corporation of the Province of Manitoba, owns and operates two casinos in the city of Winnipeg; owns and operates the provincial Video Lottery Terminal network; is the exclusive supplier of break-open tickets and bingo paper in Manitoba; and distributes and sells tickets for lotteries operated by Western Canada Lottery Corporation and the Interprovincial Lottery Corporation. The organization employs approximately 1,900 people in a variety of locations and positions across the province (Hayes, 2007).

Background

As a result of rapid expansion of MLC in the mid-1990s, many young supervisors and managers within the organization had risen through the ranks as a result of their extensive technical gaming knowledge. However, formal management training had been inconsistent and at the discretion of each department. With the arrival in 2000 of President and CEO, Winston Hodgins, a new emphasis was placed on employee development and, in particular, management development that would support an increased focus on excellence. An executive-led Management Development Committee was appointed to guide the development process.

Exhibit 7–2: Dimensions in Leadership

Competency Areas

- Teamwork and Cooperation
- Building Strategic Performance
- Self-Development and Initiative
- Achieving Quality Results
- Coaching and Developing Competency
- Communication
- Valuing Diversity
- Customer Service
- Integrity and Building Trust
- Technical/Professional Knowledge
- Leading

Dimensions in Leadership Program Overview

Based on an organizational needs assessment with input from all levels of the organization, the four-level Dimensions in Leadership (DIL) program was developed, and Levels 1 and 2 were introduced in September 2003. The DIL program was designed to build upon existing skill levels within each of (MLC defined) 11 leadership competencies (see Exhibit 7–2) and, through this program, build stronger leaders. MLC saw this as a move to increase its competitiveness. Research had identified a link between strong leadership and increased employee satisfaction, increased customer satisfaction, and increased revenues.

The DIL program incorporated many of the focus areas outlined by the needs assessment into a larger manager/supervisor development framework. In the context of the four strategic focus areas of MLC—customer, people, financial, and process—the program examined 11 specific competency areas, all of which were determined necessary for great leadership. All courses were developed to build skills based around a particular competency. Courses were designed and delivered through a combination of inside SMEs, an outside corporate training organization (Achieve Global), and two partnering universities (University of Winnipeg and University of Nevada–Reno). Participants were able to achieve success at each level and had the option of continuing with their training after Level 4, to earn a Certificate in Management from the University of Winnipeg and a Certificate in Gaming Management from the University of Nevada–Reno in addition to a management certificate from the corporation.

Training Delivery

From September 2003 through September 2004, 14 two-week training sessions (level 1 and 2) were implemented for supervisors and managers. These were linked to the development of the 11 DIL competency areas. Combined, these 14 sessions provided training to a total of 258 MLC employees from all areas of the corporation. The president and CEO, as well as the executive management team, fully supported the program and played an active role in program delivery by facilitating two half-day courses, reviewing employee development plans, and presenting certificates in each session.

Program Evaluation Process

Program evaluation was part of the initial planning process for the DIL training. Decisions regarding which areas of management competency development and business impact to study determined the data collection plan. Pre-planning for the evaluation process was critical to ensure that the necessary data were available to complete a comprehensive program evaluation. A four-step evaluation procedure, based on the four levels of evaluation model by Donald Kirkpatrick (1994), was developed to examine the impact of DIL training on MLC and its individual departments.

Each of the four levels of evaluation reflected a separate aspect by which the benefits of the program were assessed. Reaction and learning evaluations (levels 1 and 2) were used to evaluate the quality of training and the degree of learning during training as experienced by the participant. Reaction questionnaires were completed at the conclusion of each training course by all participants in attendance. Instructor observations of simulations and role plays were used to assess learning.

The transfer of knowledge, skills, and beneficial attitudes to the job (evaluation level 3) was measured by action planning and pre- and post-competency assessments. The business impact (level 4) of the training was evaluated by monitoring the organizational key performance indicators of individual departments and the total organization both pre- and post-training.

Measuring Results

Before entering DIL training, each participant was required to complete a core competency review. Participants, with the assistance and agreement of their managers, scored their current skill level on each of the 11 core competencies. Scores were assigned using a scale of 1 to 4 for managers and 1 to 3 for supervisors. Within each skill level, participants were also asked to assign themselves a skill level of developing, intermediate, or advanced. Using increments of one-third to represent the three skill degrees, participants were assigned scores based on their skill level and skill degree. This resulted in a maximum score of 3.99 (or 4) for managers and 2.99 (or 3) for supervisors. Each participant completed core competency reviews in conjunction with their immediate managers and submitted them to the Organization Development department for monitoring.

Evaluation of participant reaction and learning (level 1) was undertaken using a participant questionnaire that asked participants to score each workshop in each of six areas. Reaction questionnaires were completed at the conclusion of each training session by all participants in attendance. Instructors monitored simulated work activities and role plays, which were used in every course to identify knowledge, skills, and attitudes that participants had acquired (level 2) and thus predict the likelihood of improvements in job performance (level 3). Each individual was asked to assess his or her progress on each of the 11 competencies 12 months after completion of DIL training. Changes in competency levels were then calculated based on the difference between pre- and post-training competency scores.

Action Plans

The transfer of the new knowledge to the workplace was recorded through the use of participant action plans. Each participant developed a plan outlining specific signals that would indicate behavior change. Action plans were due on the last day of the two-week training session, and the process was monitored by personnel from the organization development area.

The action plan design, which involved selecting key areas of focus and choosing indicators of performance, was developed to resemble the performance and development program already in use at MLC. The intention was to foster an environment that encouraged a continuous improvement model for leadership development. Participants, with input from their managers, chose their own key focus areas for improvement. They were offered support and coaching to help them with the process of identifying key competencies and documenting how the competencies were learned, observed, and measured. Each individual was asked to assess his or her progress toward achieving behavior change at three time intervals: 3 months, 6 months, and 12 months following completion of DIL training.

Findings

All trainees identified their initial reaction to the training as very positive as indicated from the participant questionnaires. Participants also indicated that the workshops were effective in encouraging learning and were relevant to their positions. The overall workshop quality rating for all 14 courses in the program ranged from 4.36 to 4.95 out of 5.

On average, managers reported skill increases in all 11 competency areas. The largest increases reported by managers were in the areas of coaching and developing competency (4.07 percent increase), followed by achieving quality results and building strategic performance (2.77 percent increase in each). The smallest area of increase was reported in the area of valuing diversity (1.47 percent increase).

Supervisors reported increases on all 11 competencies on average. The largest increases reported by supervisors were in the areas of building strategic performance (6.48 percent increase) and interpersonal communication (5.85 percent increase). The smallest area of increase that was reported was in the area of leading (3.70 percent increase).

Some participants reported follow-up scores that were lower than their initial scores. This may be due to the fact that some participants may have recognized after training that their skill levels were, in fact, lower than they previously thought and together with their manager re-adjusted their skill level scores. However, overall, an increase in competency levels was reported for the managers and supervisors.

The competencies that supervisors and managers chose to target from the 11 available competencies for their development were quite evenly distributed. The area of building strategic performance was chosen the least often for closer examination by both managers (chosen by 8 percent) and supervisors (chosen by 6 percent). Six organizational key performance indicators were monitored for the 12-month period of the program evaluation for the purposes of identifying the impact of the training program on the business. The results showed a positive and significant impact on the business operation of the organization.

Although training alone cannot be fully responsible for the improved statistics, both senior management and the participants have identified the DIL training as being a strong contributor to a positive business impact throughout the organization. At the time of this study, the organization had not yet implemented an employee survey process that may have been able to further support these results.

Conclusion

The DIL program resulted in a positive impact on the leadership competency levels of 258 participating supervisory and management staff as well as a positive impact on the key performance indicators of the organization. The management development committee received substantial communication to indicate that the DIL participants have had the opportunity to apply their new classroom learning on the job in a supportive environment and to discuss challenges with their managers. Evidence of this new learning is apparent when the organizational key indicators are reviewed by senior management. Perhaps more importantly, the DIL program has provided these individuals with opportunities to increase their self-confidence in their ability as leaders. This has assisted these individuals in applying their enhanced leadership skills to situations within the workplace. In closing, it is important to comment on three key factors in the success of the DIL program, according to the participants:

▶ The comprehensive needs assessment provided many opportunities for stakeholder input and clearly identified the needs of the participants and the organization. The program design and delivery stayed true to the identified needs.

▶ A strong evaluation process that was effectively communicated in advance of the program helped participants build excitement prior to the start of the program and to continue the commitment to learning well after program completion.

▶ The strong support and involvement of the executive members of the organization in both the planning (management development committee) and the delivery of the program (executive lecturers) added the important elements of authenticity and teamwork to the program. As the vice president of Corporate Marketing & People Services observed, "We have proof DIL has not only improved managerial skills, but built bridges through all levels of the organization."

Source: Organization Development Institute: Evaluating a Leadership Development Program by Judith Hayes, pp. 89–95, 2007.

Think About This

How is the case above consistent with the approach described in the chapter? How is it different? If you believe it is different, explain the advantages and disadvantages to using the approach described in the case for competency-based training and learning.

The Bottom Line

Learning and performance professionals typically face two common situations: (1) they are handed a competency model developed by someone else and asked to use it to develop training resources; or (2) they must relate their existing slate of online and onsite courses, and other planned learning experiences, to a competency model. Many learning and performance professionals may have to do both.

In the first situation, learning and performance professionals will find that linking competencies and their behaviors to the resources needed to build those competencies and elicit those behaviors is not an exact science. They can, however, be successful if they take steps to ensure that learning resources are linked to the behavioral indicators of the competency model for each targeted group. They should not assume that traditional classroom training is always the best or the only way to build competencies; many other approaches may be used.

In the second situation, learning and performance professionals should prepare all training content in a similar format so that it may be compared. Then they should relate training content to behaviors. Next, they should relate the behaviors elicited by the existing training course to the behavioral indicators of the competency model applicable to the targeted group. Finally, they should decide whether training content should be changed to align better with the competency model or whether other approaches, apart from training, may be better to build competencies and elicit the desired behaviors.

Getting It Done

This chapter emphasized how to link training to competencies/behavioral indicators or how to link competencies/behavioral indicators to training. Here are some questions to help you develop a mindset for the application of the principles you learned in this chapter.

1. Most development occurs on the job. How could learning and performance professionals link on-the-job work experiences to competencies/behavioral indicators?

2. There might be more ways to link competencies/behavioral indicators to training than the approaches described in this chapter. Doing that may require some creativity. Can you think of other ways to link competencies/behavioral indicators to training?

The Future of Competency-Based Training and Learning

What's Inside This Chapter

In this chapter, you'll learn

▶ 10 predictions about the future of competency-based training and learning
▶ How to organize your thinking about ways to prepare to meet the challenges posed by those predictions.

This chapter offers 10 predictions on competency-based training and learning. Those predictions are listed here but are described in more detail below. In the future, competency-based learning will

▶ become more accepted
▶ focus more on differences between exemplary and fully successful performers
▶ be facilitated by technology more readily

▶ require learners to take more responsibility for their learning process

▶ require more comprehensive thinking about how to build competencies

▶ be supplemented by growing attention to ethics and values

▶ be increasingly integrated with all other components of HR management and performance

▶ require more thinking about ways to link an organization's strategic objectives, expressed in the form of a balanced scorecard, to individual competencies

▶ necessitate new ways of thinking about evaluation

▶ focus as much on functional/technical competencies as on general competencies.

Prediction 1: Competency-Based Learning Will Become More Accepted

Tradition is difficult to overcome. That is as true in the learning and performance world as it is in any other field. Training needs assessment has traditionally relied on a three-way focus on work analysis, learner analysis, and work setting analysis. The usual goal is to explore how the work is done, who will attend off-site training (and what they already know about the training topic), and where learners will apply what they have learned (how working conditions on the job will affect the ability to apply what was learned).

But learning in the modern organization requires new thinking. Gone are the days when one size fits all. Increasingly, workers select training when they want it, how they want it, and where they want it. Competency-based learning, which can be supplied in smaller, re-usable chunks, fits very well with individualized learning. In short, it includes many possible venues for learning—and thus takes a very broad view of the context in which meaningful development can occur.

Competency-based learning implies more than individual learning. Needs assessment, instead of focusing on the needs of groups of learners, requires a greater emphasis on individuals. In the past, organization training that was foisted on all employees was referred to somewhat irreverently as "sheep dip" training. Competency-based training brings increasingly scarce training resources to the persons that need it the most and avoids subjecting people to training that they really don't need, even if many others do.

Managers and learning professionals alike are becoming more aware that learning can occur in many formats and many contexts. There is growing reluctance to send people far away from work sites to participate in learning due to concerns about time away from work, travel costs, the availability of solid alternatives such as web meetings, as well as potential threats (terrorist, pandemics, etc.). Furthermore, competency-based training can lead to improvements in productivity as has been demonstrated with leadership training. Also, competency-based training integrates very well with other HR disciplines such as recruiting and selection, performance management, succession planning, and compensation. Competency development can also be linked to organization capabilities that link to organization strategy. For all these reasons, the authors predict that competency-based learning will continue its aggressive growth.

Prediction 2: Competency-Based Learning Will Focus More on Differences Between Exemplary and Fully Successful Performers

Let's determine the differences between an exemplary performer and a fully successful performer.

Indicators of an Exemplary Performer: Successfully applies this competency in the most challenging circumstances; serves as a role model for others and is a recognized resource for others when help is needed; truly excellent in all elements of this competency and consistently performs this competency at a very high level of excellence.

Indicators of a Fully Successful Performer: Willingly provides assistance and useful information to meet customer needs; takes appropriate actions to provide accurate information to customers; assumes ownership of customer issues and takes appropriate steps to correct problems.

Learning professionals know that showing results is growing more important. The days of offering learning programs merely on faith are passing away. Learning professionals must be prepared to show that what they do leads to improvements. Of course, one way to do that is to find out why some people are exemplary performers with high productivity differences over fully successful performers. That requires competency studies that pinpoint differences. Although individual differences may not answer all of the questions about why some people are more productive than others, it can explain at least some of the reasons. And although some competencies cannot easily be developed but must instead be recruited and selected, an important goal is to raise the productivity of many workers closer to the level of the best performers.

Prediction 3: Competency-Based Learning Will Be Facilitated by Technology More Readily

Technology is growing more readily available to support competency-based learning applications. Learning practitioners who read just about any training journal or who do even a minimalist search on the web will find many vendors and products available. These include programs that:

- identify competencies
- assess individuals against the behaviors linked to competencies
- list out resources to build competencies in line with performance and development gaps
- record and monitor individual development plans
- inventory the competencies available in the organization to meet special challenges or strategic objectives (so that talent can be found on a moment's notice)
- distribute learning via a variety of mobile devices
- track management decisions about how to build the competencies of high potentials, high performers and high professionals
- facilitate customization of competencies to match local culture
- collect data to evaluate results of competency-building efforts.

When competency requirements are made transparent and competency models are made available online to workers, technology can facilitate individual career planning. When competency differences between levels of the organization's hierarchy are made available to managers and individuals are assessed against them, technology can facilitate succession planning and talent management.

Competency maps, which show competency targets for different roles, organization levels, or requirements for the future, will become increasingly common in the learning field. A *competency map* illustrates where an individual is and where he or she must go to qualify for future positions (or remain in place in a current position as competitive conditions change). Competency maps may be placed online to facilitate decision-making about what individuals need to do to prepare themselves for the future or for moves to other parts of the organization.

Prediction 4: Competency-Based Learning Will Require Learners to Take More Responsibility for Their Learning Process

The half-life of human knowledge is steadily dropping. Indeed, a day will come when people graduate from a university and find that much of their knowledge is already obsolete. The World Future Society predicts that professional knowledge will soon be obsolete almost as soon as it is mastered.

Learning must shift its focus from teaching "subjects," "topics," or "courses," and begin focusing on training people to learn how to learn. More attention should be paid to learning agility, the ability to learn faster and better. Already the evidence suggests that high potentials—those who are both promotable and are outstanding performers—learn better than others who are not high potentials.

Prediction 5: Competency-Based Learning Will Require More Comprehensive Thinking About How to Build Competencies

Ask a manager how to develop workers today, and you are still likely to hear "send them to a training course." Managers still do not understand that most development occurs on the job and is integrated with the work rather than occurring in classrooms or in online workshops. Learning and performance professionals have a challenge of making managers more aware that the most effective learning occurs on the job, in real time, and as a result of the people that workers are exposed to, whom they work for, what challenges they are given, where they work, and what time pressures they face.

In the future, a combination of greater learning needs combined with a drive for cost-effectiveness will force organizational leaders to get on the bandwagon and embrace new and perhaps accelerated ways to prepare people for immediate and future challenges. Work and learning will have to be more carefully planned and integrated. Competencies will provide guidance about what learning is needed and how it can be measured.

Prediction 6: Competency-Based Learning Will Be Supplemented By Growing Attention to Ethics and Values

Traditionally, competencies have been linked to work results or productivity. But the challenges of continuing scandals—first Enron and then the financial crisis of 2008–2009—has prompted the need to take a fresh look at important criteria when recruiting, selecting, developing, and appraising workers. Is it enough to link competencies to performance? Or do we also need to devote more attention to *values* (what is regarded as good or bad) and *ethics* (what is regarded as right and wrong)? Our prediction is that the role of values and ethics will become increasingly important in the future.

Prediction 7: Competency-Based Learning Will Require More Creative Thinking About All Components of HR Management and Learning and Performance

We have already described the current move toward integrated talent management systems. At many progressive organizations, competencies are the common denominator by which all components of a fully integrated HR system are organized. Instead of using job tasks as the foundation for all HR actions, competencies have grown increasingly important because they facilitate a more holistic, accurate view of what it takes to be successful and are better adapted to a rapidly changing world. Not only will integrated talent management (with competencies as the foundation) become the norm, but learning considerations will also become increasingly pervasive in all HR decisions, including employee selection, promotion, compensation, and off-boarding.

Prediction 8: Competency-Based Learning Will Align With the Organization's Balanced Scorecard

Aligning learning with an organization's strategic objectives has long been an important goal for learning and performance professionals. However, the demonstrable link has been weak. The connection will grow and become increasingly visible. Short-term results, as measured by profitability, will be only part of the story. Learning will be designed to move the dial on additional measures, such as those suggested by the Balanced Scorecard, which establishes organizational objectives in four areas: (1) financial; (2) customer; (3) business process; and (4) learning and growth. The goal will be to create short-term and long-term results, increasing competitive advantage, and organization sustainability. Some organizations may creatively reinvent the categories of the scorecard. Furthermore, organizational goals will be more effectively driven down through the organization to all divisions, departments, and individuals. Organizational leaders will align all components of the organization's balanced scorecard objectives to individual competencies. In that way, it is clear which competencies are most critical to organizational sustainability and competitive success. Key performance essential to organizational success will become increasingly measurable, and continual learning will be an increasingly important part of the strategic equation.

Prediction 9: Competency-Based Learning Will Necessitate New Ways of Thinking About Evaluation

Traditional learning and performance evaluation methods have centered on Donald Kirkpatrick's four levels—reaction, learning, behavior, and results—or Jack Phillips' fifth level, return-on-investment. The challenge of the future is to move beyond evaluation of groups that participate in training to evaluation of individuals who participate in development—and how individual development contributes to organizational results. Results may increasingly focus not just around return-on-investment but also around the Balanced Scorecard.

Prediction 10: Competency-Based Learning Will Focus As Much on Functional/Technical Competencies as on General Competencies

Many organizations have already established general competencies so that it is clear what competency differences exist by hierarchical level. That is necessary so that succession plans and talent management programs can be properly calibrated to prepare people for possible promotion in the wake of expected waves of retirements. After all, about one fourth of all senior executives in the *Fortune 500* are retirement eligible. After years of downsizing, few middle managers are really ready for promotion, a problem only intensified by the cutbacks during the financial crisis of 2008–2009.

But attention is also shifting focus. Organizational leaders are growing more aware that, when retirements eventually occur, vital technical competence of technical workers—such as engineers, Management Information Systems professionals, HR professionals, and many others—will be lost. When they retire, they take with them institutional memory (remembrance of why and how decisions were made in the past) and proprietary knowledge (gained from their experience) about the most important operational systems in the organization. Think about what happens when an engineer retires from a high-tech firm. He or she takes away perhaps years of technical knowledge needed to acquire and sustain competitive advantage derived from specialized knowledge.

Exhibit 8–1: A Worksheet for Planning to Identify and Address Future Challenges

Directions: Use this worksheet to organize your thinking—and that of other stakeholders—about how to address possible future challenges that may affect your organization and its ability to compete in the future. Consider competency modeling as part of your thinking. For each trend listed in the left column below, indicate in the right column what specifically your organization should do to address the trend. At the bottom of the worksheet, add in your own ideas about possible future trends that may affect your organization and how your organization should address them.

Trends Competency-based learning will...	What Should Your Organization Do to Address the Trends?
1. Become more accepted.	
2. Focus more on differences between exemplary and acceptable performers.	
3. Be facilitated by technology more readily.	
4. Require learners to take more responsibility for their own learning process.	
5. Require more comprehensive thinking about how to build competencies.	
6. Be supplemented increasingly by growing attention to ethics and values.	

Exhibit 8–1: Continued

Trends Competency-based learning will...	What Should Your Organization Do to Address the Trends?
7. Require more creative thinking about all components of HR management and learning and performance.	
8. Require more thinking about ways to link an organization's strategic objectives, expressed in the form of a balanced scorecard, to individual competencies.	
9. Necessitate new ways of thinking about evaluation.	
10. Focus as much on functional/technical competencies as on general competencies.	
11. Other trends (Please specify)	

Hence, many organizations are beginning to launch knowledge transfer programs to try to capture and pass on the wisdom gained from the past. One way to do that is to focus on technical or functional competencies. And that need will only intensify globally in the future.

Conclusion

Use the activity shown in Exhibit 8–1 to organize your thinking—and the thinking of other stakeholders in your organization—about ways to address the challenges posed by these predictions. You may also use that activity to offer predictions of your own and think about ways to meet those challenges.

Getting It Done

This chapter offered some predictions about the future of competency-based training and learning. Here are some questions to help you develop a mindset for the application of the principles you will learn in this chapter:

1. How is your organization implementing competency-based thinking? Does the implementation approach(es) help prepare the organization to meet the future challenges predicted in this chapter?
2. How might "balanced scorecard" thinking be adapted to evaluating competency-based training and competency-based learning?

Appendix A

Frequently Asked Questions (FAQs) About Competency-Based Training

The authors would like to thank the members of the Chicago chapter of the American Society for Training and Development for offering the questions below. These questions are intended to reflect frequently asked questions (FAQs) that may be asked as learning and performance professionals launch a competency-based learning effort.

1. ***70/20/10 (OJT/Networking/Formal Training): Which competencies are best taught with each approach?***

   Most competencies can be taught through any of the three modalities, but may be more effectively taught through a blend of all three. For example, basic presentation skills could be taught in a classroom setting. Small groups of employees might pair off and practice presentations together in between classes. A year later, when faced with making a challenging presentation to organization executives, a coach could make very specific suggestions for how to craft this speech, as well as provide needed encouragement and confidence building.

2. *What is the role of "informal training" to address competencies?*

Informal training refers to a wide range of new learning approaches, such as coaching and mentoring, on the job training (OJT), social/collaborative learning, and more. Based on the 70/20/10 prescription, 90 percent of learning should be informal, so informal learning could be said to be the primary source for competency training. One strength of informal learning is that it can be tailored to meet individual needs. Individuals can learn anytime they want, in small or large chunks, at the pace they are capable of moving. Informal learning can be effective for many special needs in competency development. For example, coaching can be very effective for assisting a person who needs extra help, for an individual with a need to perform at an exceptionally high level of competency, or for developing a specialty in a small number of individuals when traditional training would be too expensive. Informal learning can be an extremely useful addition to competency development after some formal learning because it can help learners understand the "tricks of the trade" or tacit knowledge that may not be captured well in traditional learning.

3. *What is more effective: addressing gaps or building strengths? What are the advantages of each?*

This is a topic that continues to be debated. The correct answer probably is, "It depends." If an individual is placed in a new position, or stretched in his or her current position, then some growth in competencies will most likely be required. A person transitioning from individual contributor to supervisor is one example. If new competencies are not developed, the prognosis for future success is not good. On the other hand, focusing on strengths is often the best choice for a person who is already established in a position. For example, if you have a software developer who lacks strong self-management skills but shines when working with others, it may make good sense to continue to develop that employee's collaboration skills.

4. *How do variables such as industry or public versus private sector affect competency-based training?*

As research by ASTD and other groups has shown, industries do not invest the same amount of money on training. Generally, manufacturing firms invest the most. Government agencies and retail firms tend to invest the least. Research has explained that these differences exist, but it is open to debate as to why they do.

One reason might be the historical view in the United States—which is different than in many other countries—that business work is somehow better than government work. Another reason might possibly be that it is easier to see the tangible results of investments in manufacturing than in service firms, where results are less easily seen in measurable terms. In any case, competency-based training is likely to be adopted first in those industries that have historically prized training most and only later adopted by organizations that are less likely to invest so much in people-related issues such as government or retail firms.

5. *How do you measure competency development? How do you track it on an ongoing basis?*

   Let us count the ways. Most commonly, competency development is measured using a rating scale that might range from beginner to expert. Self and supervisors participate, and others such as peers and direct reports could too. Increasingly, certifications are developed to document the measurable demonstration of competencies. All of the traditional assessment approaches are also possibilities, such as tests, assessment centers, portfolios, review boards, and sometimes results-achieved.

6. *Should development be designed for a specific person, a specific position, or both? If for a specific position, how does one handle people who have different skill sets? For example, one employee may be a college graduate with good writing skills, while another may be someone with more experience than education.*

   Most competency development is individualized. Traditionally, the idea is to compare individuals to the competency model required for their current level on the organization chart (such as executive, manager, or supervisor) and their current level of competence. When deficiencies exist, they are called *performance gaps*. When individual abilities are compared to competency requirements for higher levels of responsibility—or higher levels of technical ability—they are called *developmental gaps*. Individual development plans (IDPs) are typically devised to narrow one or both gaps.

7. *At what point do you determine if it is feasible for an individual to develop certain competencies (especially if it is taking a lot of time or effort to develop them)? How do you determine when it is wiser to concentrate on developing people who already have their general competencies aligned with the requirements of the job?*

   This question almost answers itself. When it takes too long to develop certain competencies, it is evidence that the wrong person is in the job. (It is important to emphasize that there are no "bad people," but there *are* people who are not well suited for a specific job.) Generally, it is wise to study the people who are successful doing work and find out "what makes them tick." What is it that makes them so successful? Sometimes the answers go beyond what is typically examined in job interviews—such as appearance, interpersonal skill, educational level, and experience level. For instance, an individual who is driven to succeed and is thus highly motivated could outperform others. Profile successful people doing the work or ask people how they approach their work and what they consider important.

8. *What are the critical components of an effective development plan?*

   An effective development plan begins by pinpoint determination of the highest development priorities. Development assessments, performance reviews, or business initiatives may help to prioritize goals. Each development priority is then entered into the plan as a goal. Besides the typical elements of a goal (title, description, action steps, measures of success, and support needs) a development goal is often linked to a particular competency and development resources (for example, coaching, classes, or e-learning).

9. *How do you determine how good (for example, competent, advanced, or expert) someone needs to be on a competency?*

   This information is typically provided by subject matter experts and entered into the competency model. The desired performance level (DPL) is then selected from the competency rating scale (for example, beginner–expert). We have found that assessing a desired performance level can be done more objectively and efficiently when the needed levels are assessed for a group of jobs from a function. For example, DPLs might be established simultaneously for all marketing positions.

10. *What are the basic required steps for career planning with an employee?*

Let's define career planning as the process of considering and planning for changes (typically expansions) in one's role. Let's assume that the person has already completed competency assessments related to current as well as other positions in the company. At that point, the process may continue with the employee responding to one or several instruments that help identify personal preferences with work. Given that most companies today are not looking for their computer programmers to decide they are better suited to be artists or bakers, we typically use an assessment that measures job preferences that can be met at the company, such as preferring to work alone or in groups, whether the person likes to make decisions or not, whether he or she likes a more structured or less structured job, and so on. It is also helpful to identify demographic interests, such as in what locations or departments the person would like to work. Next, the employee searches (assisted by a coach or online tool) for positions that match personal interests and competencies. The employee is presented with as much additional information as possible about potential target positions (minimally, a job description), and then selects positions he or she would like to put into a career path. At that point, development goals are created in the Individual Development Plan to begin preparing for the new roles.

11. *A lot of employees don't know what they need to do to move into a new role. For example, a secretary wants to develop for manager of the mailroom. How do you map out the competencies and tasks to get there?*

The competencies should be mapped out in a competency model. See Appendix B on competency modeling if a competency model hasn't been created already. If you choose to certify individuals on tasks, then the job description (presuming it is up to date) of the target role should be a big help. Concentrate on the most important tasks (you can rate each task on importance and frequency and multiply the two figures together to get a weight). Save the results of your analyses so you don't have to recreate the wheel the next time someone wants to move into this role.

12. *For career management, how do you reconcile differing perspectives on the best career path for an employee? Maybe the company thinks an individual should move in one direction, while the individual has other ideas. Tension is possible.*

Career paths may be determined in more than one way. One approach is to analyze how people got where they are. For instance, what positions did the present CEO occupy on his or her way to the top? What positions did senior executives occupy on their way to the top? What do they have to say about what they learned in their previous positions that were critical to their future success, and what do they feel they lack? Another approach—and there are more than two— is to examine what career paths will most effectively develop the competencies essential to success in the organization. To determine those career paths, interview exemplary performers about their perceptions of what they learned of importance in their previous jobs or what assignments they feel will be essential to help the organization achieve its strategic business objectives.

13. *How do you manage employee resistance to reasonable career development goals and realistic career outcomes?*

Not everyone shares the opinions of others about what their potential can be. Some people see themselves as exemplary performers when nobody else does. One way to deal with that problem is to carry out a 360-degree assessment to demonstrate to people how they see themselves and how others (immediate supervisor, peers, and subordinates) regard them. That can sometimes be effective in demonstrating to people that others do not share their high opinions of themselves. A second way to deal with the problem is to give people "stretch assignments" that will reveal their own lack of ability—and perhaps dramatize it to the individuals so that they are more willing to "take coaching." Of course, with some people it will never be possible to shake their faith in themselves to the point that they are willing to be developed. They are likely to be disappointed in the future if they don't receive the promotions they desire and will probably become turnover statistics. If the organization's leaders have objectively measured them, then their loss will not be felt. But if the organization's leaders do not use objective measures of competence, it is possible that individuals who are not clones of their immediate supervisors will be unfairly assessed.

14. How should you customize competency-based learning for your organization? What are the important adjustments?

The most important adjustment is to develop relevant competency models that are measurable and that apply to the organization's unique corporate (and national) culture. It is always important to ask, "How was the competency model developed?" Since there can be a tendency to do a rush job to save time and money, some competency models are not based on the unique corporate culture of the organization. Once the competency model has been made measurable through behavioral indicators, behavioral anchors, or work outputs with quality requirements, learning and performance professionals should analyze the training and other developmental experiences by the behavioral indicators, behavioral anchors, or work outputs they are linked to. It will then be necessary to compare individuals to the competency models, identify individual gaps, and narrow those gaps through planned learning experiences that are intended to build competencies.

15. How do you prioritize competency-training needs based on individual or organization needs?

That is a tough question to answer. The reason: What matters to individuals for their own career growth may not matter to organizational leaders, and what matters to the organization's leaders may not enjoy the ownership or buy-in of individuals, who may not see "what is in it for them" to build some competencies. One way to address the problem is to identify the strategically important competencies to the organization so that it may achieve its strategic objectives. As individuals prepare their Individual Development Plans, based on competency assessments, organizational leaders can choose to fund or support those competency-building efforts that are most relevant to meeting organizational strategic objectives and make developmental resources for alternative needs that the individual finds more important than the organization available at the individual's expense. The goal is to find a way to integrate and balance individual and organizational needs.

16. How can we incorporate individual differences in how people learn into competency-based training?

A learning style represents how a learner approaches acquiring knowledge or developing a change in behavior. Each learner is motivated through different methods that influence learning performance, such as environment, psychological comfort, social styles, and profiles. Self-managed learning opportunities are an excellent way for accommodating individual differences. Does the person learn better in the morning or the evening? In one-hour or four-hour chunks? Does the person like to read a book or participate in a community of practice? These differing preferences can often be accommodated.

17. **What kinds of communications are needed prior to assessing people on competencies?**

First, it may be helpful to have a steering group with broad representation decide whether or not to assess people on competencies as well as how the assessments will be done. Next, it is beneficial for a high-level executive to send out a letter announcing the assessments and telling people why the assessments are being done. Linking assessments to organization values or continuous improvement usually is effective. The executive announcement should occur a minimum of several weeks in advance of assessments. Then, follow with a communication about details of the assessment (steps, schedule, individual responsibilities, and sources of support).

18. **Since many competency assessments are based on ratings by others, how do you help raters rate more accurately? What about replacing quantitative with qualitative scales?**

There are a number of steps that can help people rate more accurately. Begin by letting people know the purpose and uses of the assessment. If there is a lot of paranoia, it may be helpful to let individuals own their own results and share as they wish the first year. Stress the importance of frank feedback in order to get value out of the assessments. Then, if possible, give assessors some calibration training. This can be done online or in a classroom by educating people about the competencies, the rating scale, and having them practice making ratings. Sometimes assessors are required to pass a calibration test before they are allowed to make assessments.

19. **Who "owns" competency assessment data? The individual? Supervisor? What if the VP asks to see it?**

Ownership varies based on a number of circumstances as well as company preferences and culture. Competency assessments done for development purposes are *sometimes* owned by the individual, whereas competency assessments related to performance reviews are typically owned by supervisors and are visible to persons above in the organization hierarchy. Ownership can evolve over time. Ideally, you can reach a state where the data are available to all persons with a legitimate reason to have access.

20. *What kinds of competencies can be strengthened by training? Which cannot?*

Most psychologists agree that changing personality traits, particularly after the teenage years, is difficult. For example, a characteristic like "achievement motivation" may be difficult to strengthen by training since individuals who possess achievement motivation are internally driven by the need to achieve. However, this is generally the exception.

For the most part, we do believe that the vast majority of other competencies can be strengthened through training or appropriate development. Using an example of introversion and extroversion, an introverted person can be taught to give an excellent speech or to provide outstanding, warm customer service. The key is to identify the specific behaviors that are required for the trainee, and then provide the needed support that will allow the individual to exhibit the desired behaviors. You won't be turning an introvert into an extrovert, but that isn't your mission and it isn't necessary to achieve the desired performance.

21. *Beyond competencies, what "deeper characteristics" should be included in a competency model (for example, traits such as detail orientation, cheerful, or values such as integrity)?*

There isn't much question that successful performance requires certain personal characteristics, such as integrity, teamwork, and detail orientation. We have no problem with including these in job competency models so that they will be assessed regularly. Early in the journey of implementing competencies, most organizations identify core competencies and values. Core competencies are those that are expected from all employees. Ideally, these core competencies or values are consistent with organization capabilities (differentiators). For example, if innovation is a competitive advantage and part of an organization's strategy, ideally it will be included as a core competency. Many organizations select integrity as a core value. Core values might also be part of competency models.

22. *What is the right amount of competencies to select for a competency model? Three? Eight? 40? Or do you make some critical, some not?*

While many organizations seem to prefer limiting competency models to 10–15 competencies, we have seen organizations that are very successful with 20–30 competencies, which includes core competencies. The answer to this question is partially dependent on the tools you have available to manage competencies. For example, if you have software that helps you prioritize development needs, it can pick the most important three competencies for an individual to develop from a competency model of 10 or a list of 50. We do believe in assigning weights to competencies. One advantage is that it allows you to choose a subset from a competency model. It's not practical to include 30 competencies in a behavioral interview, but you could pick the five to eight competencies with the highest importance.

23. *Should competency models be built through a perceptive (SME) or empirical approach?*

The vast majority of competency models are built using input from subject matter experts. Of course, it is possible that SMEs might provide incorrect information. For example, they might identify some critical competencies that have little or no impact and they could easily fail to identify competencies that do matter. An empirical method would test whether competencies made a difference, possibly by comparing the results of persons with and without certain competencies. While additional validation of competency models would be welcome, it is hard to imagine many organizations with the resources to pursue an empirical strategy for more than possibly their core competencies. Further, there are so many variables to consider that it would be challenging to empirically test a complete competency model. Rather than discarding a perceptive approach, we recommend strengthening it. Most important, don't expect good results if you tell your supervisors to pick important competencies. We believe that you will achieve far more valid results when a trained facilitator works with SMEs.

24. *Should the competencies in a model (at least the core model) interact together to create value and achieve the strategic plan, or is it OK if the competencies are unrelated to each other?*

Some core competency models are built like a pyramid. At the base are competencies expected of all individual contributors, and employees climb the pyramid by doing more and more to facilitate the success of others and the organization overall. However, growth can also be achieved by mastering the competencies in one model and by preparing for other roles with more advanced competencies.

25. *What other HR processes "need to change" after we do competency modeling for training purposes?*

We are fans of integrated talent management efforts. That is, focus on competencies with strategic impact and apply the competencies to virtually the whole cycle of employment, starting with employee selection and finishing with off-boarding. Imagine the increased impact of training when there is a concerted effort from day one of employment to select, prepare, advance, and reward employees based on growth in a finite set of critical areas.

26. *What is the relationship between competencies and certifications? Licenses? If your employees have professional certifications or licenses already (for example, a professional pharmacist), what is the interplay of that and competencies or competency models?*

Professional certifications are similar to competency models in that they define requirements for competence. Many associations and governmental bodies have defined competence requirements (for example, ASTD has defined required competencies for a Workforce Learning and Performance professional) and where they exist, and we hardily recommend leveraging them. If an individual is renewing a certification or license every few years, then there is usually no need to include the same competencies in the competency model. A competency model will still be needed in most cases because there probably will be organization-specific competencies that are not covered by an external license or certification.

27. *What are appropriate* levels *of competence and how many should we measure? When should we use a "frequency of demonstration" scale (always or almost always) versus a level of expertise (novice, advanced, or expert)?*

Most frequently, we see organizations distinguishing and measuring between three to five levels of competence. Once you get to six or more, some individuals will have difficulty making reliable distinctions between the levels. Levels of competence are different depending on whether the rating is one of development level or job performance. In other words, someone may have the competence to do a job satisfactorily (he or she has developed the necessary competencies) but that doesn't necessarily determine his or her actual performance. For the purposes of trainers, developmental assessments are usually most important. We have seen organizations successful with a scale such as beginner, novice, skilled, advanced, and expert. Sometimes organizations like to use a simplified variant of Bloom's learning levels (knowledge, comprehension, application, analysis, synthesis, and evaluation). Frequency scales (rarely, sometimes, usually, almost always, and always) are appropriate for competencies that are less a matter of skill and more a matter of willingness or volition, such as integrity or customer focus.

28. *What is the relationship between how competencies are used for development purposes versus performance reviews? For promotion?*

For performance reviews, we assess whether an individual has met expectations. For development, we look at the current development level as well as the development target. For promotion, it would be wise to look at both competence and actual performance.

29. *What are the* ethical *responsibilities of the competency-based trainer? For example, what about maintaining confidentiality in assessment data, keeping confidences when employees divulge information, and giving employees frank feedback?*

The first and most important ethical responsibility of a competency-based trainer is to ensure that people are being fairly and objectively measured. A good competency model should be developed by some investigation of the unique characteristics shared by successful or superior performers. But sometimes people are tempted to take shortcuts that result in competency models that do not reflect the unique context of a corporate culture. Competency-based trainers also have the responsibility to maintain confidentially when it was promised to people, use competency results in the ways that employees were told they would be used, avoid any discriminatory intent or impact from the use of competency data, keep confidences, and give frank feedback.

30. *What are the most commonly required competencies and why are they the most common?*

In a study several years ago, the Corporate Leadership Council found that the following were among the most common competencies: integrity, drive, interpersonal skill, learning agility, strategic thinking, flexibility/adaptability, self-confidence, getting results, customer focus, decision making, and teamwork. We aren't personally aware of a more recent study, and we can verify that these competencies are still in widespread use. These competencies are common both because they apply to virtually all employees and because organizations review the competency models of other organizations when creating their own.

31. ***How do you communicate to managers and train them so that they can effectively support competency-based training?***

When competencies are first introduced in an organizational setting, it should be considered a major change in corporate culture. Managers and workers alike will require continuing training and information about what competencies are, how they compare to job descriptions, why they are worth using, how they are used by the organization, how they are measured, and much more. The most important thing is to maintain an active, continuous communication and training effort so that key stakeholders are reminded of what competencies are, why they are used, and how the organization and its individuals are benefiting from the use of competencies.

Appendix B

Competency Modeling: The Basics of Identifying Competencies

A competency model (see chapter 1) is a set of competencies (typically 10 to 30) that describe the capabilities of successful performers. Critical competencies are identified by knowledgeable persons called subject matter experts (SMEs). Competency models are at the foundation of training and more generally talent and performance management. By focusing on the behavior of successful performers in addition to the KSAs required to perform the responsibilities listed in a job description, we identify critical capabilities that otherwise would not be apparent. Considering the behaviors of effective performers adds an empirical (data-based) element to competency modeling that is likely to provide us with more accurate and comprehensive models than if we just brainstorm about what characteristics may be important to perform a duty.

Potential Benefits of Creating Competency Models

Competency modeling requires a significant investment of time and effort. Fortunately, the potential benefits are substantial. From the standpoint of the organization, competency modeling facilitates

- hiring productive employees (or contractors) that are a good fit with the organization and that are likely to have a lower turnover

▶ conducting high-quality, targeted individual and group training needs analysis because we can more accurately determine training gaps

▶ creating individual development plans (IDPs) for current positions

▶ creating career plans for future positions

▶ identifying the most promising candidates for promotion

▶ creating succession plans and evaluating bench strength

▶ developing workforce plans to have the needed talent to meet future needs (e.g., enough nurses to meet the demands of an aging population)

▶ restructuring an organization and "right-sizing."

In conjunction with job analysis, competency modeling can

▶ update or create an understanding of key job responsibilities, job deliverables, essential tasks, education and experience requirements, job task weights, and compensable factors ratings (used in determining appropriate wages or salaries)

▶ identify job characteristics that help determine whether a job matches the personal preferences of an individual, probable levels of job satisfaction, and likelihood of turnover

▶ define job standards that can be used similarly to goals in performance plans as well as performance reviews.

Types of Competency Models

Competency models range in their coverage from narrow to broad, from a single task to the jobs of everyone in a large organization. All of the following types of competency models have value depending on circumstances:

▶ task model (e.g., telephone sales)

▶ job or role model (e.g., customer service representative)

▶ job family model (e.g., sales)

▶ job-level model (e.g., for all individual contributors)

▶ talent pool model (e.g., high potentials)

▶ core competency model (e.g., competencies such as integrity or innovation that applies to all employees in the organization).

One level of a competency model (such as core competencies or job family competencies) often is used as a starting point for developing other competency models (such as job competency models) more quickly and more consistently.

In practice, the techniques used to develop the different types of competency models are similar, although the number of persons providing input to the model may differ. Dozens of persons may participate in the development of organization core competencies. Senior leaders typically are involved, and all employees may have the opportunity to comment. By contrast, one to three individual contributors may be the SMEs providing input required for a job competency model.

Types of Competencies

Models are typically constructed from three types of competencies:

- ▶ Core competencies: These are competencies and values that are considered critical for all persons within an organization. Competencies such as innovation, integrity, customer focus, and safety are common. Some organizations also identify leadership core competencies that are required of all persons with direct reports.
- ▶ Cross-functional competencies: These are competencies that are important for persons in many, widely varying job roles. Competencies such as budgeting, time management, and strategic planning are examples.
- ▶ Professional–technical competencies: These are competencies that pertain to the essence of a role, such as marketing, IT, or security. Examples are marketing research, C++ programming, and criminal behavior knowledge.

Elements of a Competency and a Competency Model

Currently, no single standard exists for a competency or a competency model. Consequently, competency models vary greatly in their contents, quality, and sophistication. To clearly define each competency, we find value in the following competency components:

- ▶ Competency number: This identifier makes it easier to find a competency in a large library. In addition, the number can indicate which competencies are closely associated. That is, competencies 603 and 607 may both be part of a group of project management competencies.
- ▶ Competency name: Teamwork, integrity, heavy water chemistry (used in fossil fuel power generation), and so on.
- ▶ Competency description: One to three sentences describing the area.

▶ Behaviors: Four to 10 observable behaviors that are examples of what a strong performer might do.

Competency models benefit from some additional elements:

▶ Competency rank or weight: Some competencies are more important than other competencies and receive higher weights, particularly in the context of a specific role or job. Weights typically add to 100 percent. For example, one competency might have a 60 percent weight, another could be weighted at 25 percent, and another 15 percent.

▶ Desired performance level (DPL): In the context of a particular job, the required level of expertise will vary. You may need individuals in one role to be experts at written communication, whereas beginning skills may be sufficient for another role.

Creating a Competency Model During Job Profiling

We recommend that competency models be created as part of a broader job profiling process. A job profile is a type of job description that contains a number of elements in addition to the competency model. There are three primary reasons why a competency model by itself is not enough:

▶ To accurately evaluate which competencies are important for what role, we need to clearly understand the tasks, outputs, or deliverables that are expected from an individual in the role.

▶ Being able to associate required competencies to specific tasks or required deliverables may be important for establishing the validity of personnel decisions such as hiring or promotion decisions. This association is sometimes referred to as "job relatedness." Tying competencies to other elements enhances the legal defensibility of an organization's actions.

▶ As stated above, competency models help drive good decision making such as hiring, prioritization of training needs, and career development. Even better decisions can be made when additional information is considered, and some of this additional information can be efficiently collected from SMEs while collecting information about competencies. For example, whereas job competencies should help us understand if an individual is prepared to perform a role well, it will not tell us whether a person is comfortable or enjoys the role. In other words, we need more than just competency models to establish good job fit.

Although content of the job profile is likely to be customized somewhat for each organization, a typical job profile may include

▶ Basics: Name, a job code if desired, code, SMEs providing input, date created
▶ Requirements: Education, experience, certifications, and so on
▶ Responsibilities: Typical tasks or outputs and importance
▶ Competency model: Competencies, competency weights, and DPL for each competency (from novice to expert)
▶ Job characteristics: Elements of the job such as decision making, interaction with others, administration, pace, physical tasks, interaction with others, and so on.

Given their many uses and benefits, as well as being essential to competency-based training, competency models are probably the most important single element of job profiles.

Approaches for Collecting Job Profile Information

Ideally, job profiling should be one of the first steps in developing a learning and talent management process. When job profiling isn't done well, all subsequent steps are at risk. For example, using the wrong competencies to select or develop employees for a position wastes time, and worse, may mean you select an unqualified employee or miss an opportunity to provide critical training. There are even potential legal consequences if job profiling is not done well and in accordance with applicable legal requirements outlined by the Equal Employment Opportunity Commission's 1978 EEOC Uniform Guidelines.

There are a variety of ways to collect information for job profiles. We have seen all of the following approaches used, but with varying degrees of success:

▶ small group meetings with SMEs
▶ individual interviews
▶ supervisor-selected competencies
▶ employee surveys
▶ consultant generated models
▶ professional association or industry-developed models
▶ public agency–developed models
▶ competency card sorts.

Although we don't believe there is one method that is best for every organization or situation, we generally have seen the best results come from structured, small group meetings of two to four SMEs led by a person trained in competency modeling and group facilitation. The SMEs do not necessarily need to be physically co-located: web-based meetings can be effective and also allow access to diverse SME groups.

There may be temptation to not engage a trained facilitator and instead leave job profiling or competency modeling to supervisors or an employee survey, but we discourage either of these approaches. When you create a job profile and identify the critical competencies, there are rules that help determine whether a competency should be selected. A trained facilitator adds a great deal to the process by skillfully applying the rules and following a structured process. For example, there is little value in selecting a competency (such as basic reading skills) if job entry requirements are likely to screen out anyone who can't read. Even if supervisors or employees were trained to develop job profiles, the task is likely to take a backseat to their regular job duties and be completed without the care and reflection that is required. Given that learning and talent management rest heavily on the foundation created by a job profile, you should not risk building a structure on a weak foundation.

Using small, facilitated groups—although effective—can be a time-consuming and expensive option. Fortunately, there are many strategies for stretching your resources.

▸ One of the best ways to reduce the time to create a job profile is to begin with a template that can be tailored for specific roles. You can create a job profile for a functional area or department, such as accounting, and then build all your accounting job profiles by taking what is relevant from the department profile.

▸ Developing core (for everyone) employee competencies and core leadership competencies saves time as certain competencies are used in all job profiles. A core set of competencies can also be developed for each function:

▸ Working with experienced SMEs speeds up the process significantly. After going through the structured process one to two times, the SMEs can drive the process and cut the required time by 25 percent or more.

▸ Hybrid approaches may be used. For example, the facilitator can prepare a draft job profile and present it to SMEs. Alternatively, SMEs may be asked to complete questionnaires before the meeting, such as selecting critical competencies. Hybrid approaches can shorten the facilitated meeting by 50 percent.

▶ Using web or other meeting technologies can reduce travel time and costs.

▶ Job profiling can be spaced out over several years. There is nothing wrong with beginning with a relatively small number of job profiles and expanding over time.

Validation of Competency Models

Competency model validation seeks to show, from a practical, research, statistical, or legal standpoint, that a competency model is accurate.

You can use many approaches to validate competency models. The most common are

▶ using SMEs to identify critical competencies

▶ associating competencies to job tasks or job deliverables—by associating competencies, you are demonstrating job relatedness

▶ passing draft competency models to others within your organization for comment and revision

▶ having the same competency models developed by independent groups and then comparing and contrasting the results

▶ benchmarking the competencies you have selected against other competency models from consulting companies, industry groups, best-in-class organizations, or competitors

▶ correlating performance reviews to competency scores

▶ conducting concurrent or predictive validation studies and using statistical analyses to show a significant relationship between your selected competencies and a criterion measure such as job performance.

It is useful to distinguish between practical validation, empirical validation, and legal validation, although they overlap. Whereas as having a colleague review a competency model might be practical, empirical validation may require rigorous studies by qualified researchers, and legal requirements require adherence with relevant statutes.

Remember that competency models may form the basis for many important decisions such as employee selection, promotion, and possibly termination, so you may be required to develop your competency models in a manner that could withstand legal challenges. For example, in the United States, the EEOC Guidelines of 1978 define legally acceptable types of validity. Unless your intended use of competency models is very narrow, they should be developed in a manner that the decisions made from them are consistent with applicable legal requirements. If you are not certain about whether there are applicable laws in your area, it would be wise to investigate further.

Conducting empirical research is rarely a practical option. Such studies tend to be time-consuming, expensive, and not necessarily persuasive to corporate citizens. And yet, if in the future we can find practical ways to scientifically validate competency models, great benefits could ensue. Imagine being able to concentrate your learning efforts on a short list of five or fewer competencies that account for 80 percent or more of success in a role. Properly validated models provide power and efficiency à la the Pareto Principle of identifying the 20 percent with 80 percent of the impact.

Although arranging for extensive reviews of competency models by others in your organization may be politically required or may help build consensus, it can double your effort and rarely adds much to the quality of competency models. It also might not make the model any more valid or legally defensible. Reviewers typically do not have the benefit of working with the trained facilitator who helped SMEs develop the first draft with SME input.

Appropriate competency model validation can also differ based in part on the type of competency model you are creating. For example, it may be appropriate to invest more effort on validating a core competency model since its use will be pervasive in your organization. You might compare it to numerous benchmarks, such as the models of best-in-industry or best-in-class firms, consulting firm studies, and academic research. By contrast, validation of an individual job model may be based primarily on the use of SMEs for input as well as association of the competencies to job tasks.

Bottom line, it is to everyone's advantage to have valid competency models. You will want to focus your learning and training efforts on the highest priority areas. Although all the differing types of validation can be bewildering, fortunately the same types of practices that give you confidence in your competency models, such as SME input and job relatedness, also tend to provide legal defensibility. Furthermore, efforts can be spaced out over time, and competency models need to be maintained to stay up-to-date. You ideally will need to fine-tune your competency models by reviewing them at least every two to three years. When you review and update your models, consider what competencies proved to be important since the model was last revised, and this also will validate your models. Finally, you can keep alert to opportunities that may arise to use more rigorous validation approaches for your most important competency models.

Qualities of a Competency Modeler

Creating competency models requires several skill sets. First, competency modelers need to be good listeners. They need to be able to absorb and understand information that may sometimes be foreign to them (for example, when creating a model for a technical area in which they have little or no expertise). They also need to display good active listening skills so that SMEs feel their input and effort is worthwhile.

Group facilitation skills are also required. Typically, the competency modeler must lead a small group of individuals, produce a quality product, move the group quickly, and stimulate the group when it tires. It may be necessary to deal with tricky situations such as drawing out some SMEs that are either quiet or reluctant to risk disagreeing with their boss or more senior SMEs. Competency modelers must inspire confidence, a sense of purpose, and feelings of accomplishment.

Most individuals can pick up the competency modeling process quickly. We recommend

> ▶ orientation to the process through presentation and discussion of material such as that in this appendix
> ▶ observation of an experienced competency modeler
> ▶ creation of one to two competency models with an experienced modeler assisting
> ▶ creation of one to two competency models with an experienced modeler present to observe and provide feedback after the meetings.

Tailoring Your Job Profiling Process

Within the guidelines of good competency modeling practice, there are many ways to tailor the process to your own circumstances and preferences. To design a process that is best for you, we recommend

> ▶ Identify a steering group as well as an implementation team. Often there is some overlap in these groups
> ▶ Meet with key stakeholders for the process. Typically, this includes members of leadership, training, organizational development, recruitment,

compensation, succession planning, performance management, and representatives from line functions. Interview and do focus groups with stakeholders to determine interests and needs.

▶ Determine the strategy for developing the profiles based on stakeholder needs. Principal options include:

- Build the profiles using SMEs in small group meetings that are led by a trained competency modeling facilitator.
- Have qualified competency modelers build draft profiles for your organization based on existing materials and then bring in SMEs to tune-up and validate the draft. This approach makes good use of limited SME time.
- Use an expedited approach that pre-associates competencies to common, basic job functions, such as delegating, analyzing, working with numbers, and so on. Then, work with SMEs to verify which job functions (and therefore which competencies) apply.
- Purchase a database of competency models to use as a foundation. This may get you up and running most quickly and minimize your internal effort, but it can be costly and the models may not be a very good fit with your positions.

▶ Decide on which basic elements of the competency modeling process you wish to include now and which you may want to add later. For example, performance standards may not be needed, or it may be that determining desired competency performance levels will be an enhancement for the second year.

▶ Determine what special information collection needs your organization has that go beyond basic competency models. For example, do you need to collect information to evaluate job pay and create internal equity? Do you want to use the process to update your job descriptions? Do you want to identify entry requirements such as education and experience? Leverage your competency modeling efforts, if possible, to collect additional useful information.

▶ Identify what organization information is currently available and pertinent to the profiling process such as job descriptions, performance standards, and so on.

▶ Tailor the elements of your process further:

- Use a pre-developed commercial competency library, an internal competency library, or a combination of both. If you are planning to use more than core employee and leadership competencies, developing your own comprehensive library can be very time-consuming. In that case, using a commercially available library may be your best bet. Be sure to eliminate or deactivate competencies that are not needed by your organization. Also, it is likely that you may need to add at least a few organization specific competencies not found in a commercial library or to re-write competency descriptions.
- Decide if you want to capture job responsibilities, deliverables, or both to define the job.
- Decide whether you will give importance weights to job tasks and competencies, and if so, how these will be determined.
- Select the job characteristics you will use (attributes that affect whether an individual will be engaged and satisfied with his or her work). These can be derived from a commercially available list or an internal list. These characteristics should usually have some proven usefulness in career development and talent management.

  ▷ If not previously done, identify employee core competencies. Core competencies apply across the organization and are key to success in every position.

  ▷ Identify core leadership competencies for all persons that lead others.

Creating core competencies will typically involve many others, including senior leadership. It is very important to follow a careful process for creating them that usually relies on research, review of competencies of other companies, significant input from organization members, and communication/change management strategies.

Job Profiling Meeting Steps

We recommend you follow 10 steps for job profiling and competency modeling. As we said previously, this is certainly not the only way to create competency models. We can say that we and others have successfully used this approach (with some fine-tuning) to create thousands of competency models.

This approach relies on one to two small group meetings with SMEs. Typically, the first competency-modeling meeting includes Steps 2–8. Steps 9–10 are optional and generally occur in separate meetings. The time estimates for each step are a rough guideline. Actual times vary based on whether up-to-date job descriptions exist, the complexity of the job, the number of SMEs, personal style, and the meeting facilitator. However, as evidenced by the allotted time, the major focus of the meetings is on creating the competency model.

Step 1: Pre-Meeting Preparation

It is not surprising that proper meeting preparation goes a long way to ensuring successful job profiling, and it will be difficult or impossible to bring back a group of SMEs if a meeting doesn't succeed. See Appendix B, Exhibits 2 and 3 for a review of meeting preparation steps.

Step 2: Starting the Meeting

In addition to the typical introductions of participants, we find it useful to give participants a quick preview of the meeting by reviewing the primary steps of the process (see Appendix B, Exhibit 1).

Step 3: Put Job Tasks into Task Groups

The next step is to insert (or modify) the job task groups and job tasks (or job roles or key deliverables, depending on your preferred approach). A range of five to 15 tasks is customary, but at times, more or less may be appropriate. Select a task group title and enter the appropriate tasks in each group.

Step 4: Assign Weights to Task Groups

Next, weight task groups. Percentages are OK, but the Casio-Ramos (CR) estimation approach is better. With CR, the total points don't have to add to 100, and it is easier to give accurate weights than with traditional percentages. To use CR, give 100 points to the most important task group and weigh the other groups relative to the first group. For example, a task group that is half as important would get 50 points. If you wish, convert back to percentages after completing the CR weights, but that isn't necessary.

Step 5: Select Competencies

Next, select competencies from your competency library. Generally, we recommend 15 to 35 competencies in total. This step is one of the most important in the whole process and can take 1/4–1/3 of the meeting time. We suggest having the SMEs move from one competency group to another rather than considering each competency one by one or considering the whole competency library all at once.

It is important that the facilitator keeps the group from choosing too many competencies. When selecting critical competencies, the saying "less is more" applies. Pick the 20 percent of competencies with 80 percent of the impact. Before you select a competency for a particular competency model (unless it is a core competency), be sure that the answer is "yes" to these five questions:

- ▶ Is the competency critical to successful performance on the job?
- ▶ Is it difficult, time-consuming, or costly to train people that do not have this competency?
- ▶ Is this competency used often enough to be considered significant?
- ▶ Do job incumbents have some difficulty with this competency? In other words, is this competency often a development priority?
- ▶ Is this competency significantly different from other competencies you have selected?

Sometimes you will find that your library is missing critical competencies needed for the job you are profiling. In that event, you will need to add to your library.

Step 6: Link Competencies to Task Groups

Linking competencies to task groups is an effective way of ensuring the competencies selected are valid and increase legal defensibility. To link competencies to task groups, identify where competencies are used in the job. For example, suppose that you have four task groups (task groups A–D) and you want to link the competency "teamwork." Possibly teamwork is important when performing the tasks in Task groups A and C, but teamwork may not be critical for the tasks in groups B and D.

Step 7: Create and Fine-tune Competency Weights

Weighting of competencies is optional, but it does yield benefits. Knowing the most important competencies will help you determine training needs, select employees, and establish legal defensibility of the competency model.

Determining the relative importance and ranking of competencies is not simple. If two to three SMEs are asked to rank competencies, they often will not agree. One logical way to rank competencies is to assign weights based on the competency links to task groups (see previous section). For example, suppose teamwork is linked to task group A and task group C. If task group A was weighted at 100 points and task group C at 50, then teamwork has 150 points and teamwork can be ranked versus the other competencies. Calculating the percentage weight is also easy. Simply total

Appendix B Exhibit 1: Key Steps in the Competency Modeling Process

Below is a 10-step process that you can use to build a competency model. *Note:* Bolded steps are those that we think are essential. Italicized tasks add value, but could be skipped.

1. **Pre-Meeting Preparation**	(20–60 minutes)
2. **Review and Revise Job Task List**	(10–20 minutes)
3. **Put Job Tasks into Task Groups**	(5–10 minutes)
4. *Assign Weights to Task Groups*	(5 minutes)
5. **Select Competencies**	(30–45 minutes)
6. **Link Competencies to Task Groups**	(10–15 minutes)
7. *Create and Fine-tune Competency Weights*	(5–15 minutes)
8. *Select Job Characteristics*	(10 minutes)
9. *Set Desired Performance Levels*	(30–90 minutes)
10. *Develop Job Performance Standards*	(30–120 minutes)

all the points, and then divide the weight of each competency by the total of the weights. For example, 150 divided by a total of 1,000 points would yield a 15 percent weight.

Adding up the points is a good starting point, but we also ask SMEs if they wish to make a few adjustments to the rank order and weight of the competencies. Typically, the competency weights will fall into three to four different levels. For example, there might be several competencies at 7.5, 5.0, and 3.0 percent. If one competency looks too high or low, it can be moved up or down one or two levels.

Step 8: Select Job Characteristics

Completing job characteristics is optional but useful. SMEs are asked to provide information on aspects of the job that affect how much an individual will like a job. For example, is there job variety? Is the job slow or fast paced? The job characteristics matched with the preferences of the individual can be used to make better career development or succession planning decisions. With this information, an employee will know competency gaps (i.e., can they do the job?) as well as job characteristic gaps (whether the job fits with their personal preferences).

Step 9: Select Desired Performance Levels (DPLs)

This step is also optional, but it increases the predictive power of a competency model. To understand DPLs, imagine that a scale such as the following is used to evaluate a competency such as *project planning*:

1 = No knowledge
2 = Beginner
3 = Competent
4 = Advanced
5 = Expert

It would be erroneous to simply assume that a training gap exists because someone is rated a 3 out of a possible 5. Some jobs may require beginner knowledge, while others could require advanced or expert knowledge. By identifying the desired performance level, we can more accurately determine if a training gap exists.

Step 10: Develop Job Performance Standards

If desired, job standards may be developed for each task group. Job standards are typically used to help define acceptable performance. Therefore, they can be used to evaluate training effectiveness, for certification, or as a component of performance reviews. We recommend that you have your SMEs focus on the performance or behaviors of outstanding performers when writing job standards. We use brainstorming questions such as:

- ▶ What does it mean to be outstanding at . . . ?
- ▶ Think of the best person you ever saw at this task group. What do they do that leads you to say they are the best?
- ▶ What does it mean to "go the extra mile"?

Appendix B Exhibit 2: Preparation for Job Profiling

A. Select profiling participants

Selecting the right participants is very important. Typically, one to three job incumbents are involved, as well as one to two supervisors. Job incumbents selected should have significant experience, and they should be successful performers. We recommend two to five SMEs. Larger groups may be used, but our experience is that the end result is no better, more time will be required to complete the steps, and more resources are being expended.

B. Review technical competencies

If not completed previously by someone in the department, one of the senior SMEs should be asked to review the technical competencies (in their functional area) in the competency library. The SMEs may want to add some competencies or make other modifications.

C. Obtain job descriptions or other descriptive job information prior to the meeting

D. Update job tasks prior to the meeting

It is a good idea to have the SMEs review job descriptions prior to the meeting. Particular attention should be given to the list of job responsibilities. The intent is to have an accurate list of job responsibilities for the job profiling session so that appropriate critical competencies can be selected. Therefore, obsolete responsibilities should be eliminated from the list and critical job responsibilities should be added. It is also useful to identify a list of primary job deliverables. We find five to 15 key responsibilities to usually be sufficient for most jobs. If the organization wishes, this process can be used to update job descriptions while creating the profile. Alternatively, the job task list can be created or revised during the SME meeting, but it is generally time intensive.

E. Identify generic task group titles

Greater efficiency is achieved in the competency modeling process if we group key job responsibilities into two to six task groups. If possible, generic task groups (typically four to five) should be selected prior to the first competency modeling meeting and used as appropriate (with modifications allowed) for all job-profiling meetings. This adds consistency to the profiles and avoids duplicate work. For example, we find that most tasks can be organized into the following task groups: Professional/Technical, Project or Program Management, Administrative, Communication, Customer Service, Managing People, and Business Development.

F. Prepare the meeting room (or web meeting)

We find it most efficient to capture results using a software package designed to do job profiling. This obviously requires an online connection in the meeting room. Arrange for a computer projector. It is helpful to have a printer so that copies of the work can be handed out to participants during or after the meeting. A flipchart will also be useful.

Appendix B Exhibit 2: Continued

G. Begin the competency model

Before the meeting, we suggest that the competency modeler identify the job responsibilities and prepare them for presentation to SMEs. In addition to reducing meeting time, this further familiarizes the facilitator with the job.

H. Circulate pre-meeting communications

Send participants the pre-meeting memo, competencies list, tips for picking competencies, a description of the rating scales (if selecting desired performance ratings), and job characteristics. Have copies on hand for the meeting. You may also want to have examples of completed Competency Models on hand. See Appendix B Exhibit 3 for a sample pre-meeting communication memo.

Additional Pointers

Learning to do competency modeling is not difficult for most people, but being good at it requires effort. The two primary concerns are collection of valid data and effective group (SME) facilitation to keep the team motivated, satisfied, and productive. An effective facilitator adds a great deal to the success of the process.

To collect valid information, the facilitator must be prepared to gently challenge SMEs. Given the propensity for SMEs to select too many competencies, the facilitator may want to question whether the competency matches the competency selection criteria described earlier. The facilitator can also add value by asking about certain competencies that appear to be relevant and have not been selected. Finally, the facilitator can enhance quality by ensuring that the group is thorough as it steps through the process. As the pacesetter, the facilitator should continue the discussion for each step until confident that the identified information is solid.

Leading a SME group effectively always benefits from solid group facilitation skills. There is a lot of ground to cover in a job-profiling meeting. It is critical that the facilitator keeps the meeting moving along at a brisk pace while ensuring the collection of high-quality data. The facilitator naturally must draw out reticent participants while gently quieting those that might dominate. There are often status differences and participants with supervisor/subordinate relationships, and these must be handled skillfully to ensure subordinates are participating freely.

Appendix B Exhibit 3: Sample Job Profiling Memo for SMEs

XYZ Job Profiling

MEMO

To: XYZ Participants in Job Profiling

From: Nathalie Jones & Peter Smith

Date: May–July, 2010

Re: Job Profiling Sessions

INTRODUCTION TO JOB PROFILING

What it is

Job profiling is a process for identifying required competencies and technical skills for different jobs at XYZ.

Why

XYZ is creating a customized and comprehensive talent management system.

Job profiling (including Competency Models) is the foundation we need for talent and performance management. Job profiling provides data that will help employees prioritize areas for development for present and future positions. In addition to career development, job profiling provides critical information for employee hiring, succession planning, 360-degree feedback reviews, and sometimes performance reviews.

Benefits

Talent management systems provide employees with high-quality tools that can help them be more successful with their current responsibilities as well as providing a basis from which to grow and qualify for successively more rewarding responsibilities and positions.

XYZ can benefit from talent management in many ways:

1. Increasing individual accountability for performance
2. Fostering a more positive culture throughout the organization
3. Empowering individuals to plan and advance their careers
4. Identifying best qualified persons to fill critical positions
5. Improving capabilities to effectively develop internal talent
6. Developing capability to find necessary talent for projects or committee assignments
7. Fostering diversity advancement throughout the organization
8. Attracting talented employees
9. Retaining talented employees
10. Responding today to anticipated staffing shortages or needs of the future.

Appendix B Exhibit 3: Continued

What will be happening and when

- SMEs will be selected for each job profiling meeting. SMEs are persons that are knowledgeable about a specific job, such as an experienced person doing the job and a supervisor of persons in the position.
- SMEs will be asked to provide information on one or more jobs. We will allow 1.5 to 3 hours to complete job profiling meetings, which is typically the time needed to collect the extensive information we need to fully understand a job.

Preparation Needed

- If no job description currently exists for your job (you will be notified if this is the case at the time your meeting appointment is scheduled), please prepare a list of the primary job tasks associated with the job being profiled. In general, the list should include five to 15 key tasks. Submit the list of tasks at least 48 hours before the meeting, if possible. Here are examples of job tasks:
  - ▶ Launches and manages employee performance review process.
  - ▶ Visits regional offices on a quarterly basis to promote XYZ marketing program.

Handouts for Use Before and During the Meeting

1. Introduction to Job Profiling
2. Job Task Group Definitions
3. Job Characteristics

If you have any questions or need additional information, please do not hesitate to contact your HR and training representatives.

Job Profiling Meeting Steps

Typically, a job profiling meeting includes Steps 1–7. Steps 8–9 are optional and typically occur in separate meetings. The time estimates for each step are a rough guideline.

1.	Review and Revise Job Task List	(10–20 minutes)
2.	Put Job Tasks Into Task Groups	(5–10 minutes)
3.	Assign Weights to Task Groups	(5–10 minutes)
4.	Select Competencies	(30–45 minutes)
5.	Link Competencies to Task Groups	(10–15 minutes)
6.	Create and Fine Tune Competency Weights	(5–15 minutes)
7.	Select Job Characteristics	(10 minutes)
8.	(Optional) Set Desired Performance Levels	(30–90 minutes)
9.	(Optional) Develop Job Performance Standards	(30–120 minutes)

Appendix B Exhibit 3: Continued

Competency Selection Guidelines

When selecting critical competencies, the saying "less is more" applies. Pick the 20 percent of competencies with 80 percent of the impact. As a rule, you should select a total of 15 to 30 critical competencies (including core competencies).

Before you select a competency, be sure that the answer is "yes" to these five questions:

1. Is the competency critical to successful performance of the job?
2. Is it difficult, time-consuming, or costly to train people who don't have this competency?
3. Is this competency used often enough to be considered significant?
4. Do job incumbents have some difficulty with this competency? In other words, is this competency often a development priority?
5. Is this competency significantly different from other competencies you have selected?

Job Characteristics

This rating form is to identify the degree to which a job is characterized by each of the following characteristics. These characteristics describe the environment in which job incumbents operate, and are the types of factors that may affect job satisfaction. There is no one "best" job environment; please be frank in your ratings to ensure their usefulness.

Now, for each of the job characteristics that follow, circle the number on the 5-point scale that best describes the level of that job characteristic for this job. These ratings should reflect the job as it is today, not as you would like it to be. Be sure to circle one of the numbers on the 5-point scale, not the space between the numbers.

A. Independence

LOW						HIGH
Most decisions made must first be approved by others before action can be taken.	1	2	3	4	5	Most decisions made can be implemented without prior approval from others.

Example 1: A Basic Competency Model for a Carpenter

Suppose a company needs to hire a carpenter. What kinds of competencies would be required? The fact is that "carpenters" can actually do many different tasks. The U.S. Department of Labor defines a variety of different carpenters, including construction carpenters, rough carpenters, drywall installers, wood model makers, cabinet makers, and more. The same differentiation occurs with most job titles. That is part of the reason it is essential to identify job tasks before selecting competencies.

Let's assume that we want to define competencies for a construction carpenter. Using the structured approach defined above, the result might be something similar to that shown in Appendix B, Exhibit 4. Depending on the nuances of the job, the model for a construction carpenter will likely vary from company to company.

Example 2: A Two-Level Competency Model for Senior Executives

Competency models can be built in a manner that relates competencies to each other. For example, the Senior Executive Service of the U.S. government has defined a leadership competency model with five "executive core qualifications" (ECQs). ECQs have between four and six competencies each. The ECQs are

- ▸ ECQ1: leading change
- ▸ ECQ2: leading people
- ▸ ECQ3: results driven
- ▸ ECQ4: business acumen
- ▸ ECQ5: building coalitions.

The competencies for ECQ1, leading change are

- ▸ **Creativity and Innovation**
  Develops new insights into situations; questions conventional approaches; encourages new ideas and innovations; designs and implements new or cutting edge programs/processes.
- ▸ **External Awareness**
  Understands and keeps up-to-date on local, national, and international policies and trends that affect the organization and shape stakeholders' views; is aware of the organization's impact on the external environment.
- ▸ **Flexibility**
  Is open to change and new information; rapidly adapts to new information, changing conditions, or unexpected obstacles.
- ▸ **Resilience**
  Deals effectively with pressure; remains optimistic and persistent, even under adversity. Recovers quickly from setbacks.

Appendix B Exhibit 4: Competency Model for a Carpenter

	Competency Number	Competency Name	Weight	Task Groups [ ] View Details			DPL
1	2801	Detail Orientation	8.5	☑A	☑B	☑C	Default ▼ Default: 5 – Always
2	2821	Achievement Orientation	8.5	☑A	☑B	☑C	Default ▼ Default: 5 – Always
3	17503	Basic Carpentry	8.5	☑A	☑B	☑C	Default ▼ Default: 5 – Always
4	406	Creates a Mental Picture	6.1	☑A	☑B	☐C	Default ▼ Default: 5 – Always
5	304	Arithmetic Computation	6.1	☑A	☑B	☐C	Default ▼ Default: 5 – Always
6	1006	Equipment Base	3.7	☑A	☐B	☐C	Default ▼ Default: 5 – Always
7	15613	Selecting Proper Tools	3.7	☑A	☐B	☐C	Default ▼ Default: 5 – Always
8	15701	Fitting and Assembling	3.7	☑A	☐B	☐C	Default ▼ Default: 5 – Always
9	1201	Organizational Safety Complience	3.7	☑A	☐B	☐C	Default ▼ Default: 5 – Always
10	159901	Setting Up Machines	3.7	☑A	☐B	☐C	Default ▼ Default: 5 – Always
11	15902	Checking Machines	3.7	☑A	☐B	☐C	Default ▼ Default: 5 – Always
12	15904	Removing Materials	3.7	☑A	☐B	☐C	Default ▼ Default: 5 – Always
13	15905	Removing Equipment	3.7	☑A	☐B	☐C	Default ▼ Default: 5 – Always
14	15906	Cleaning Equipment	3.7	☑A	☐B	☐C	Default ▼ Default: 5 – Always
15	15908	Adjusting Machines and Tools	3.7	☑A	☐B	☐C	Default ▼ Default: 5 – Always
16	15903	Safety Checking Machines	3.7	☑A	☐B	☐C	Default ▼ Default: 5 – Always
17	15603	Trimming Parts	3.7	☑A	☐B	☐C	Default ▼ Default: 5 – Always
18	17604	Plastering	3.7	☑A	☐B	☐C	Default ▼ Default: 5 – Always
19	17605	Hanging Drywall and Paneling	3.7	☑A	☐B	☐C	Default ▼ Default: 5 – Always

Appendix B Exhibit 4: Continued

	Competency Number	Competency Name	Weight	Task Groups View Details	DPL
20	17612	Woodworking and Carpentry	3.7	☑A ☐B ☐C	Default ▼ Default: 5 – Always
21	15606	Reading Blueprints	2.4	☐A ☐B ☑C	Default ▼ Default: 5 – Always
22	15807	Visually Inspecting	2.4	☐A ☑B ☐C	Default ▼ Default: 5 – Always
23	15812	Inspecting Fixtures	2.4	☐A ☑B ☐C	Default ▼ Default: 5 – Always

▶ **Strategic Thinking**

Formulates objectives and priorities, and implements plans consistent with the long-term interests of the organization in a global environment. Capitalizes on opportunities and manages risks.

▶ **Vision**

Takes a long-term view and builds a shared vision with others; acts as a catalyst for organizational change. Influences others to translate vision into action.

Example 3: A Three-Level Competency Model for Learning Professionals

Consider the model that ASTD has developed for workforce learning and performance (WLP) professionals. According to ASTD:

The ASTD WLP competency model for learning and performance was derived from an in-depth, comprehensive study of the learning profession. The model identifies the roles, areas of expertise, and foundational competencies for professionals in the learning and performance field.

At the top of the competency model are four roles, or lenses through which WLP practitioners may view the model. Roles are groupings of targeted competencies. An individual's job may encompass one or more roles. The four roles are

▶ learning strategist
▶ business partner
▶ project manager
▶ professional specialist.

Appendix B Exhibit 5: ASTD WLP Competency Model

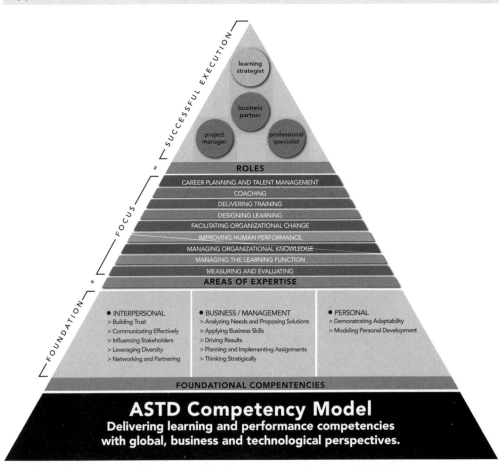

Source: Copyright © 2008 American Society of Training and Development (ASTD)

Next are areas of expertise (AOEs). AOEs are the specialized knowledge/skills an individual needs to perform in a learning and performance role. An individual may need expertise in one or more areas. ASTD has identified nine areas of expertise deemed critical for WLP professionals:

- ▶ career planning and talent management
- ▶ coaching
- ▶ delivering training
- ▶ designing learning
- ▶ facilitating organizational change

- ▶ improving human performance
- ▶ managing the learning function
- ▶ managing organizational knowledge
- ▶ measuring and evaluating.

Finally, ASTD defines foundational competencies. These are required competencies for learning and performance professionals. These competencies are categorized into the following three groups:

- ▶ Interpersonal: How well you work with, manage, and influence people, policy, and change.
- ▶ Business and Management: How well you analyze situations, make decisions, and implement solutions.
- ▶ Personal: How well you adapt to change and make personal decisions to enhance your career.

Good Competency Models Continue to Evolve

An old competency model is about as useful as an out-of-date job description. Competency models can evolve in comprehensiveness or be updated to reflect current needs. Sharp Electronics Corporation is a good example:

Sharp Electronics Corporation was an early adopter of competency models. Sharp initially developed a core competency model. Seven years later, it decided to embark upon a second phase. Phase 2 included five competency models that are specific to several strategically important job functions in sales and marketing. It also included a revision of the original core competency model. The plan for the third phase is to integrate the models into selection, promotion, and performance management procedures and decisions.

Part of the challenge of competency modeling is proceeding in accordance with the company's culture, needs, and resources, and all of these need to be considered when designing a competency modeling process. Organization variations will affect many design decisions, for example:

- ▶ creating a few general or many role specific competency models
- ▶ selecting SMEs
- ▶ leveraging SMEs versus pre-developed content
- ▶ use of the competency models, such as for training, employee selection, succession, compensation, or some combination

- ▶ including or discarding parts of the competency modeling process, such as competency weighting, desired performance levels, or association of competencies to tasks
- ▶ developing associated talent management components, such as assessments or development resource guides
- ▶ determining whether to create competency models using internal or external facilitators and internal or commercial competency libraries
- ▶ determining the role of technology in the competency modeling process
- ▶ creating the schedule and approach for updating competency models.

Common, carefully implemented change management practices, including involvement of sponsors and important constituents, will help determine appropriate approaches. No two organizations are likely to follow the exact same path. We strongly encourage that adjustments be made to fit your circumstances. We also suggest that you adequately pilot-test your approaches before a broader roll-out and continue to fine-tune your processes based on lessons learned and as conditions change.

About the Authors

William J. Rothwell, PhD, SPHR, is professor of learning and performance in the Workforce Education and Development program, Department of Learning and Performance Systems, at The Pennsylvania State University, University Park campus. In that capacity, he heads up a top-ranked graduate program in learning and performance. He has authored, co-authored, edited, or co-edited 300 books, chapters, and articles—including 64 books. Before arriving at Penn State in 1993, he worked 20 years as a training director in government and in business. He has also worked as a consultant for more than 40 multinational corporations—including Motorola, General Motors, Ford, and many others. In 2004, he earned the Graduate Faculty Teaching Award at Pennsylvania State University, a single award given to the best graduate faculty member on the 23 campuses of the Penn State system. His train-the-trainer programs have won global awards for excellence from Motorola University and from Linkage Inc. His recent books include *Effective Succession Planning*, 4th ed. (AMACOM, 2010), *Practicing Organization Development*, 3rd ed. (Pfeiffer, 2010), the *Manager's Handbook for Maximizing Employee Potential* (AMACOM, 2010), *Basics of Adult Learning* (ASTD, 2009), *HR Transformation* (Davies-Black, 2008), and *Working Longer* (Amacom, 2008). He was a major researcher for the last three international competency studies of ASTD, including *ASTD Models for Human Performance* (2nd ed., 2000), *ASTD Models for Workplace Learning and Performance* (1999), and *Mapping the Future* (2004). A frequent international conference keynoter and seminar presenter, he can be reached by email at wjr9@psu.edu.

Source: John Timmerman

James Graber, PhD, organizational psychologist, is managing director of Business Decisions, Inc., Chicago, Illinois, a company he founded in 1981. During his 30 years of consulting, he has worked for more than 100 domestic and international clients, including organizations such as McDonalds, United Airlines, Panasonic, General Motors, Abbott Labs, the U.S. Navy, the City of Chicago, and for numerous clients in Australia, Europe, South America, Asia, and the Middle East. He specializes in the areas of Competency Modeling, Talent and Performance Management, 360-degree Multi-Rater Assessments, Training Needs Analysis, Employee Development, Career Planning, Succession, and Workforce Planning. Jim has been involved with the development of talent and performance management software since 1992 and has served as the content expert for the *focus* talent management software suite since 1995. He has taught at four universities and has had numerous publications and conference presentations. James earned his bachelor's degree from the University of Michigan and his PhD in psychology from Claremont Graduate University in 1980.

References and Resources

Alldredge, M. E., & Nilan, K. J. (2000). 3M's leadership competency model: An internally developed solution. *Human Resource Management, 39*(2 & 3), 133–145.

Ambient Insight Research. (2009). Learning and performance technology research taxonomy. Retrieved from www.ambientinsight.com

American Society for Training & Development (ASTD). (2009). Learn from the BEST 2009, Reliance Industries, Limited, Talent Transformation Initiatives. *T+D Magazine*. Retrieved October 2009, from http://www.astd.org/TD/

American Society for Training & Development (ASTD). (2009). *2009 state of the industry report*. Alexandria, VA: ASTD Press.

Ash, R. A., Battista, M., Carr, L., Eyde, L. D., Hesketh, B., Kehoe, J., Pearlman, K., Prien, E. P., Sanchez, J. I., & Schippmann, J. S. (2000). The practice of competency modeling. *Personnel Psychology, 53*(3), 703–740.

Bersin & Associates. (2007). *The learning content maturity model: Developing a framework for integrated training and knowledge management.*

Bersin, J. (2009, October). The checklist for modern enterprise learning: Staying current in fast-changing markets. *Chief Learning Officer*.

Boyatzis, A. R. (1982). *The competent manager: A model for effective performance*. New York: John Wiley & Sons, Inc.

Bright, A., Gowing, M. K., Gregory, D., Patel, R., & Rodriguez, D. (2002, Fall). Developing competency models to promote integrated human resource practices. *Human Resource Management, 41*(3), 309.

Brown, J. (2009). *Mobile Learning 101*. ASTD TechKnowledge Conference. Retrieved January 28, 2009, from http://tk09.astd.org/sessionhandouts.html

Campbell, A., & Luchs, K. (1997). *Core competency-based strategy*. Florence, KY: Delmar Cengage Learning Business Press.

Cohen, D. (2001). *The talent edge: a behavioral approach to hiring, developing, and keeping top performers*. New York: Wiley & Sons, Inc.

Competency management: Cracking the code for organizational impact. *T+D Magazine*. Retrieved June 2008, from http://store.astd.org/Default.aspx?tabid=167&ProductId=19148

Davenport, R. (2005). Why does Knowledge Management still matter? *T+D Magazine*. Retrieved February 2005, from www.astd.org/TD/

DePree, M. (2004). *Leadership is an art*. New York: Broadway Business.

Derven, M. (2008). Lessons learned: Using competency models to target training needs. *T+D Magazine, 62*(12), 68.

Dubois, D., and Rothwell, W. (2004). *Competency-Based Human Resource Management*. Palo Alto, CA: Davies-Black Publishing.

Dubois, D., and Rothwell, W. (2004). Competency-based or a traditional approach to training? *T+D Magazine, 58*(4), 46–57.

Dubois, D. D. (1993). *Competency-based performance improvement: a strategy for organizational change*. Amherst, MA: Human Resource Development Press.

Dubois, D. (1998). *The competency casebook*. Amherst, MA: Human Resource Development Press.

Dubois, D. (1997). *The executive's guide to competency-based performance improvement*. Amherst, MA: Human Resource Development Press.

Dubois, D., & Rothwell, W. (2004). *Competency-based human resource management*. Palo Alto, CA: Davies-Black Publishing.

Dubois, D., & Rothwell, W. (2000). *The competency toolkit*. 2 vols. Amherst, MA: Human Resource Development Press.

Ey, P. E. (2006). *A track-by-level approach to performance competency modeling*. Touro University International.

Feeney, M., & Krieger, D. (2007). *Developing job-specific learning programs*. Infoline, no. 250711. Alexandria, VA: ASTD Press.

Francois, V., & Harzallah, M. (2002). IT-based competency modeling and management: From theory to practice in enterprise engineering and operations. *Computers in Industry, 48*(2), 157–159.

Gebele, S. (Ed.) (1999). *Successful executive's handbook*. 2nd ed. Minneapolis: Personnel Decisions, Inc.

Gebele, S. (Ed.) (2004). *Successful manager's handbook: develop yourself, coach others*. 7th ed. Minneapolis: ePredix.

Gilbert, T. (2007). *Human competence: engineering worthy performance*. Tribute edition. San Francisco: Pfeiffer & Co.

Goldsmith, C., Hodges, K., Martin, J., & Parskey, P. (2004). Looking in the mirror: performance improvement for performance improvers. *International Society for Performance Improvement, 43*(2), 36–43.

Grigoryev, P. (2006). Hiring by competency models. *Journal for Quality & Participation, 29*(4), 16–18.

Hall, C. (2009). Proven KM strategies: Five best practices that ensure Knowledge Management success. Retrieved October 14, 2009, from www.inquira.com/resources_articles.asp

Hayes, J. (2007). *Evaluating a leadership development program.* Organization Development Institute.

Hirschman, C. (2008). Building the bench. *Human Resource Executive, 22*(8), 35–37.

Howard, C. (2007). The learning content maturity model: Developing a framework for Integrated Training and Knowledge Management. Bersin & Associates Research Report. Retrieved November 1, 2009, from www.bersin.com

Johnson, C. (2008). Thinking differently about mobile learning. *ASTD Learning Circuits.* Retrieved October 1, 2009, from http://www.astd.org/lc/2008/0908_johnson.html

Kahane, E. (2008). Competency management: Cracking the code for organizational impact. *T+D Magazine, 62*(5), 70–76.

Kanaga, K. (2007). Performance test: Designing an effective competency model. *Leadership in Action, 27*(4), 7–10.

Kirkpatrick, D., & Kirkpatrick, J., (2006). *Evaluating training programs: The four levels*, 3rd ed. San Francisco: Berrett-Koehler.

Krieger, D., & Feeney, M. (2006). From basic competencies to job specific curriculums. *ASTD Links, 5*(8).

Krompf, W. (2007). *Identify Core Competencies for Job Success. Infoline*, no. 250712. Alexandria, VA: ASTD Press.

Laff, M. (2008). Emotional notions. *T+D (Training and Development) Magazine, 62*(2), 12–13.

Lamoureux, K. (2009, October). Experiential learning: Make it the core of the LD program. *Leadership Excellence, 26*(10), 10.

Lievens, F., & Sanchez, J. I. (2007). Can training improve the quality of inferences made by raters in competency modeling? A quasi-experiment. *Journal of Applied Psychology, 92*(3), 812–819.

Lucia, A., & Lepsinger, R. (1999). *The art and science of competency models: pinpointing critical success factors in organizations.* San Francisco: Pfeiffer & Co.

Mallon, D. (2009). Providing learning at the speed of the business: Using an integrated rapid e-Learning development and virtual classroom platform. Bersin & Associates Research Report. Retrieved November 1, 2009, from www.bersin.com

Mallon, D., Bersin, J., Howard, C., & O'Leonard, K. (2009). Learning management systems 2009: Facts, practical analysis, trends and provider profiles. Bersin & Associates Research Report. Retrieved November 1, 2009, from www.bersin.com

Metcalf, D. (2008). mLearning Quickstart Workshop. ASTD TechKnowledge Conference, February 21, 2008.

Mirabile, R. J. (1997). Everything you wanted to know about competency modeling. *T+D Magazine, 51*(8), 73.

Montier, R., Alai, D., & Kramer, D. (2006). Competency models develop top performance. *T+D Magazine, 60*(7), 47–50.

Morrison, M. (2007). The very model of a modern manager. *Harvard Business Review, 85*(1), 27–39.

Paquette, G. (2007). An ontology and a software framework for competency modeling and management. *Educational Technology & Society, 10*(3), 1–21.

Prastacos, G. P., Soderquist, K. E., & Vakola, M. (2007). Competency management in support of organizational change. *International Journal of Manpower, 28*(3/4), 260–275

Randstad Human Capital Survey. (2008). Retrieved December 1, 2008, from www.randstadusa.com

Riermeier, M., & Zimmerman, T. (2005). Creating a business-focused IT function. *Strategic HR Review, 4*(6), 28.

Robertson, I., Gibbons, P., Baron, H., MacIver, R., & Nyfield, G. (1999). Understanding management performance. *British Journal of Management, 10*(1), 5–12.

Rothwell, W. (2010). *The manager's guide to maximizing employee potential.* New York: AMACOM.

Rothwell, W. (2002). *The workplace learner: how to align training initiatives with individual learning competencies.* New York: AMACOM.

Rothwell, W., Butler, M., Maldonado, C., Hunt, D., Peters, K., Li, J., & Stern, J. (2006). *Handbook of training technology: an introductory guide to facilitating learning with technology—From planning through evaluation.* San Francisco: Pfeiffer & Co.

Rothwell, W., & Kazanas, H. (2004). *Improving on-the-job training: How to establish and operate a comprehensive OJT program.* 2nd ed. San Francisco: Pfeiffer & Co.

Rothwell, W., & Kazanas, H. (2008). *Mastering the instructional design process: A systematic approach.* 4th ed. San Francisco: Pfeiffer & Co.

Rothwell, W., & Lindholm, J. (1999). Competency identification, modeling and assessment in the USA. *International Journal of Training and Development, 3*(2), 90–105.

Rothwell, W., Prescott, R., & Taylor, M. (2008). *Human resource transformation: Demonstrating strategic leadership in the face of future trends.* San Francisco: Davies-Black Publishing.

Salopek, J. (2008, August). Keeping it real. *T+D Magazine.* Retrieved October 1, 2009, from www.astd.org/TD/

Sanghi, S. (2003). *The handbook of competency mapping: understanding, designing and implementing competency models in organizations.* London, UK: Response Publishing.

Schoonover, S. C. (2000). HR competencies for the new century. Retrieved October 19, 2009, from http://www.schoonover.com/pdf/HR_Competencies_for_the_New_Century_Final.pdf

Schweyer, A., Newman, E., & DeVries, P. (2009). *Talent management technologies: A buyer's guide to new, integrated solutions.* Washington, DC: Human Capital Institute Press.

Seema, S. (2009). Building competencies. *Industrial Management, 51*(3), 14.

Spencer, L., & Spencer, S. (1993). *Competence at work: models for superior performance.* New York: John Wiley & Sons, Inc.

Stines, A. C. (2003). Forecasting the competencies that will define "best-in-class" business-to-business market managers: An emergent delphi-hybrid competency forecasting model. ProQuest Dissertations and Theses.

Standaert, C. (2008). ArcelorMittal: Speaking the language of business. *Chief Learning Officer, 7*(6), 60–61.

Thompsen, J. (2006). Aligning content strategies with workforce competencies. *Chief Learning Officer, 5*(4), 54–58.

Wood, R., & Payne, T. (1998). *Competency-based recruitment and selection.* New York: John Wiley & Sons, Inc.

Websites

Epocrates. (2009, October). http://www.epocrates.com/products/

http://74.125.93.132/search?q=cache:tPwv3nJiHpMJ:training.fema.gov/EMIWeb/downloads/CharlesSturtULunn.doc+competency+model+examples&cd=19&hl=en&ct=clnk&gl=us — A competency model for the Education Training and Development Field used by FEMA

http://books.google.com/books?id=YTHeqeXn9ewC&dq=Achieving+the+Perfect+Fit&printsec=frontcover&source=bl&ots=u68UTQUTbY&sig=aiUC_1qcvKQQUmBW2Jj-tCUqIM0&hl=en&ei=45ncSsH9D5PGMZqT8d8H&sa=X&oi=book_result&ct=result&resnum=2&ved=0CBAQ6AEwAQ#v=onepage&q=&f=false — An online book called Achieving the Perfect Fit by authors Boulter, N., Dalziel, M., & Hill, J.

http://careerclusters.org/resources/pos_ks/FoundationKSCharts/2008/
IT-102-KSCHART.pdf — An actual competency model of sort, IT career cluster of knowledge and skills required for the field

http://edweb.sdsu.edu/people/arossett/pie/Interventions/career_1.htm — An overview of what competency modeling is, how to develop models, and use them in your organization

http://joshbersin.com/2007/12/13/wow-performance-management-really-matters-in-retail/
— A brief excerpt related to Bersins Talent Management Database supporting competency modeling for the retail industry

http://portal.cornerstones4kids.org/content160.html — Links to pdfs & word documents with example competency libraries/models and instructions on how to build ones of your own

http://techcompetencies.com — Links that can lead you to find other resources on competency modeling and competency libraries

http://thecfoalliance.org/files/2009/04/talent_management_state_of_the_industry.pdf — A section on page 5 gives information on how competency models are misunderstood and misused

http://www.astd.org/NR/rdonlyres/8643DEC9-306B-4634-A661-281EC2DF49FE/0/
010942ChapCompModelUpdate.pdf — Competency Model for Chapter or Association Leaders

http://www.astd.org/NR/rdonlyres/B922E7D3-8155-4451-B5C9-E5C0DA4401E6/0/
SanDiegoStrategicModel.doc-2009-10-14 — ASTD Competency Model for Work learning and performance specialists

http://www.astd.org/NR/rdonlyres/77858E92-6BA1-4150-8649-44B5013C9BD8/0/
Infosys.pdf — Brief overview of Infosys programs for building employee competencies. ASTD Learn from the Best, 2008.

http://www.astd.org/NR/rdonlyres/2B14FBA9-D13B-4303-8858-E66705292A37/0/
KeepingitRealcolumnAugust2008TDarticle.pdf — "Keeping it Real." ASTD White Paper on keeping Workplace Learning and Performance Competency model current, 2008

http://www.astd.org/NR/rdonlyres/1A99E24F-4BD4-4473-89DE-01ECE3CF0108/0/
RILRefinery_handouts.pdf — ASTD Learn from the Best, 2009, Reliance Industries, Limited, Talent Transformation Initiatives

http://www.bersin.com/Research/Content.aspx?id=136&fid=6832 — Highlights Bersin's competency management; link includes research reports, research bulletins, webinars, and PowerPoint presentations

http://www.britishcouncil.org/teacherrecruitment-recruitment-policy-competencies.htm — British Council's website which provides key indictors they use for recruitment and to describe their jobs

http://www.brown.edu/Administration/Human_Resources/downloads/CompetencyAssessmentDictionary.pdf — A competency model assessment dictionary

http://www.careeronestop.org/COMPETENCYMODEL/learnCM.aspx — Competency Modeling Clearinghouse competency modeling details, additional resources here to help in building a competency model as well as a review of the literature supporting competency modeling

http://www.careeronestop.org/CompetencyModel/search.aspx — A website where you can enter specifications into various fields and get more information on competency model resources

http://www.careeronestop.org/competencymodel//modelFiles/Comm.%20Computer%20Sys%20Prog.pdf — a Career Field Education and Training Plan for Communication-Computer-Systems Programming used by the US Air Force includes various competency models for different levels

http://www.cica.ca/service-and-products/business-opportunities-for-cas/primeplus-frasl%3B eldercare-services/item10444.aspx — Chartered Accountants of Canada, AICPA's PrimePlus/ElderCare Competency Model and Self-Assessment Tool

https://www.cs.state.ny.us/successionplanning/workgroups/competencies/competencies3comp.html — This link has a compiled list of links/resources that will aid you in building a leadership/management competency model

http://www.financialcareers.gov.ab.ca/competencies/finance_model.html — Government of Alberta, Financial Community Competency Model

http://www.hrsg.ca/index.php?sctn=4&ctgry=55 — HRSG —Website contains software to build fully-integrated competency software

http://www.hrtools.com/insights/chris_wright/competency_modeling.aspx — A brief blurb about identifying key abilities and writing competencies in terms of measurable outcomes

http://www.humancapitalinstitute.org/hci/tracks_competencies_top_talent.guid%3Bjsessionid=C91FFEDFB8A97D0E218265787AE2321C?_currentTab=_researchTab — A long list of competency modeling white papers and articles from The Human Capital Institute

http://www.humancapitalinstitute.org/hci/events_webcast_archive.guid?_trainingID=908 — A webcast by The Human Capital Institute that covers how successful organizations have implemented an effective competency-based talent management system

http://www.imeche.org/NR/rdonlyres/24F2E8C8-A65F-439B-8795-4383655391FF/0/
REFCompetenceStatement.pdf — Engineering Competence in the UK Rail Industry

http://www.msha.gov/inspectors/inspectorcompetencymodel.pdf — A competency model
for Mine Safety Inspector/Specialist used by the U.S. Department of Labor

http://www.opm.gov/studies/transapp.pdf — A competency model for HR Professionals

http://www.plateau.com/pdf_wp/Competency_MgtWP.pdf — Support for why competency modeling is important within an organization

http://www.talentmgt.com/talent.php?pt=s&sid=215&mode=preview — An article from
the Talent Management Magazine on competency modeling

http://www.talentmgt.com/talent.php?pt=s&sid=254&mode=preview — Another article
from the Talent Management Magazine on competency modeling

http://www.trainingreference.co.uk/news/itp070330.htm — UK publishes IT Professional
Competency Model

http://www.vanguardcanada.com/LeadershipCompetencyPowrie — An article entitled The
Leader-Manager Competency Model For The Ontario Public Service

http://www.wfm.noaa.gov/pdfs/CompetencyModel/Leadership_Mgmt_Model.pdf — A
leadership and management competency model used by NOAA

http://www.workitect.com/building_competency_models.php — Live workshops that teach
you how to build competency models

http://www.workitect.com/pdf/Competency_Dictionary.pdf — Fleshed out competency
dictionary from the company called Workitect, has a strong model of behaviorally
anchored competencies

http://www.workitect.com/competency_systems.html — Workitect — Website contains
free forms—Individual Development Plan and a competency project planning form.

http://www.wrmtraining.com/wrm/ — Competency cards

Index

THE ***ASTD*** MISSION:

Through exceptional learning and performance, we create a world that works better.

The American Society for Training & Development provides world-class professional development opportunities, content, networking, and resources for workplace learning and performance professionals.

Dedicated to helping members increase their relevance, enhance their skills, and align learning to business results, ASTD sets the standard for best practices within the profession.

The society is recognized for shaping global discussions on workforce development and providing the tools to demonstrate the impact of learning on the organizational bottom line. ASTD represents the profession's interests to corporate executives, policy makers, academic leaders, small business owners, and consultants through world-class content, convening opportunities, professional development, and awards and recognition.

Resources
- *T+D (Training + Development)* Magazine
- ASTD Press
- Industry Newsletters
- Research and Benchmarking
- Representation to Policy Makers

Networking
- Local Chapters
- Online Communities
- ASTD Connect
- Benchmarking Forum
- Learning Executives Network

Professional Development
- Certificate Programs
- Conferences and Workshops
- Online Learning
- CPLP™ Certification Through the ASTD Certification Institute
- Career Center and Job Bank

Awards and Best Practices
- ASTD BEST Awards
- Excellence in Practice Awards
- E-Learning Courseware Certification (ECC) Through the ASTD Certification Institute

Learn more about ASTD at www.astd.org.
1.800.628.2783 (U.S.) or 1.703.683.8100
customercare@astd.org

080615.31410